PITTSBURGH THEOLOGICAL MONOGRAPH SERIES

General Editor

DIKRAN Y. HADIDIAN

2

THE FUTURE OF THE CHURCH

*The theology of renewal of
Willem Adolf Visser't Hooft*

THE FUTURE OF THE CHURCH

The theology of renewal of
Willem Adolf Visser't Hooft

FRANÇOIS C. GÉRARD

PICKWICK PUBLICATIONS
An imprint of *Wipf and Stock Publishers*
199 West 8th Avenue • Eugene OR 97401

Pickwick Publications
An imprint of Wipf and Stock Publishers
199 West 8th Avenue, Suite 3
Eugene, Oregon 97401

The Future of the Church
The Theology of Renewal of Willem Adolf Visser't Hooft
By Gerard, Francois C.
Copyright©1974 Pickwick Publications
ISBN: 0-915138-01-8
Publication date 1/1/1974

Willem Adolf Visser't Hooft

Photo JOHN TAYLOR
World Council of Churches
Geneva   Switzerland

To my friends.

ACKNOWLEDGEMENT

I am deeply grateful to the authorities of the World Council of Churches who granted me a research scholarship in 1970 and opened to me the archives of their library. I should like also to express my gratitude to Dr. Visser't Hooft who showed interest in my study, gave me access to some of his files and agreed to write the preface to my book.

Geneva College, Beaver Falls, Pennsylvania contributed a travel grant in 1970 for which I am very appreciative. The inspiration and insight of my friends in Geneva, Switzerland, Hartford and Pittsburgh kept me going, I hope in the right direction. To all I am truly indebted.

Finally, I should like to express my gratitude to Miss Janice Shuler, a student at Geneva College, who typed the manuscript.

Preface

It is useful, though not always pleasant, to see ourselves as others see us. In this particular case the experience is encouraging, for I am glad to find that the author of this study has come to the conclusion that the theme of "renewal of the church" is the thread of Ariadne running through the labyrinth of my many writings on a great variety of ecumenical subjects.

The ecumenical movement was never concerned with unity alone. Since the days of the pioneers ecumenical workers have known that to unite the churches-as-they-are is not worth the trouble. Unity is only desirable as an expression of a deep transformation of the churches, in other words as the outcome of their common renewal. A united church is not necessarily a renewed Church. But real renewal must lead to unity. For genuine renewal means the rediscovery of the fundamental mandate of the church and that mandate includes to live as the reconciled people of God.

That is why I am grateful that Dr. Gérard has highlighted what I have tried to say about the emanating of church renewal and about its urgency. I know that to-day many wonder whether the old dry bones of institutional Christianity will ever come to life again. But Christians believe that Pentecost is not merely a historical event to be commemorated It is a contemporary event wherever men and women recognize the active presence of the Holy Spirit.

W. A. Visser't Hooft

TABLE OF CONTENTS

	Page
ACKNOWLEDGEMENTS	viii
PREFACE	ix
INTRODUCTION	1

CHAPTER I. THE NEED FOR RENEWAL
-Christianity as its own Adversary-

    The Decline of Christianity 9

    The Temptations of the Church--The Periods of Marriage, Tolerance, and Rivalry 15

    The Hope of the Gospel 30

CHAPTER II. THE FOUNDATION OF RENEWAL
-The Kingship of Christ-

    Of the Necessity of Meeting with Jesus Christ 44

    The Humanity of Jesus Christ 52

    Jesus Christ the Reconciler 55

    The Kingship of Christ 60

CHAPTER III. THE WAY OF RENEWAL
-The Threefold Calling of the Church-

    Conditions for Renewal 74

    Renewal in the Life of Israel and of the Church 77

    The Characteristics of a Renewed Church . . 87

        - The Church is to be in Christ 87

        - The Church is 'in via' 90

        - The Church is to Serve Man 94

        - The Church is to be Independent of the World 99

CHAPTER IV. RENEWAL AND UNITY
              -The Church as an Ecumenical Society-

              The Problem   104

              The Conflict of Ecclesiologies   109

              The Meaning of Unity   117

              Unity and Liberty 129

              Unity and Pluralism 132

              The Ecumenical Society   144

CHAPTER V.   RENEWAL AND WHOLENESS
              -The Christian and the Church-

              The relationship of Renewal and Unity to
              Wholeness 151

              The Wholeness of the Christian   153

              The Wholeness of the Church 169

CONCLUSION   181

ENDNOTES   190

LIST OF ABBREVIATIONS   231

BIBLIOGRAPHY   232

INTRODUCTION

Willem Adolf Visser't Hooft has come now to the end of a long and rich career, first as a Y.M.C.A. secretary, then as Secretary of the World Student Christian Federation, and as first General Secretary of the World Council of Churches. Indeed, it is still too early fully to appraise the significance of his contribution to the life of the Church of the twentieth century. Nothing, to my knowledge, has been written to analyse his thought or to define his influence. A series of essays entitled The Sufficiency of God[1] constitutes a testimonial to Visser't Hooft rather than a systematic study of his theological endeavor. The eminence of the contributors, however, indicates the high esteem in which theologians and Churchleaders of all traditions hold the former General Secretary of the World Council of Churches.

I owe much to that series of essays. By emphasizing the 'Sufficiency of God', this publication has helped me to see Visser't Hooft--the churchman--in a clearer light. Robert C. Mackie tells us that Dieu le veut is a favorite quotation of his friend.[2] This, I think, is a key to the understanding of Visser't Hooft. Essentially he is a Christian leader, whose thought and action have always been for him the expression of his obedience to God. God wills, creates and governs the Church. It is not in man's power to determine its course.

Visser't Hooft, as a theologian, may be open to new ideas; but his concept of man's dependence upon God remains unchanged. God comes first. He reveals Himself in Scripture. Visser't Hooft challenges the Church to read the Bible not 'historically' or 'critically', not 'egocentrically' or 'piously', but 'theocentrically'.3 The ecumenical movement is concerned with God and the discovery of His will for the renewal and unity of the Church. In re-affirming God's sovereignty, the Church will find its wholeness. God's purpose is revealed to man in Jesus Christ. Hence, the 'Kingship of Christ' becomes the root-idea of Visser't Hooft's concept of renewal; and his theology is a theology of renewal.

The whole purpose of the present study is to demonstrate that Visser't Hooft's theology is a theology of renewal. As ecumenical statesman he is obviously concerned for Church unity; it will be shown here that for him the only way to Church unity is Church renewal. The notion of renewal is the central theme of W. A. Visser't Hooft's thinking. The present exposition of his theology is primarily a delineation of this central theme. It is not my intention here to examine the concept of renewal in the thought of other theologians either for purposes of independent analysis or comparison. My task is limited to Visser't Hooft's work. Furthermore, although Church renewal may be viewed as an aspect of ecclesiology--referring to the action of the Holy Spirit in the life of the Christian community--this is not a study of ecclesiology per se. I do not set out to define Visser't Hooft's concept of the Church, but instead focus attention on the question to which he addresses himself, the question of authenticity. That is, how can the Church be the Church anew? How can it truly be the people of God in our time? How can it be faithful to the 'given' of its experience? What is the future of the Church? These are basic problems of renewal. Visser't Hooft's treatment of these problems is the subject of my inquiry.

I shall not attempt to follow Visser't Hooft in the complex unfolding of his long mandate as General Secretary of the World Council of Churches. Visser't Hooft, the churchman, was and remains in action what the theologian has become in his understanding of Christianity. This aspect of his career, however, has already retained the attention of Visser't Hooft in his autobiography.[4]

A profound interest in biblical standards of renewal came first in the theological awareness of Visser't Hooft; biblical studies gave him a new vision of the character of God and a new understanding of the crisis of human life, and determined the nature of his theology. So strong is the theocentricity of his thought, that he has been accused of dogmatism, intransigence and narrow-mindedness. His collaborators, however, recognize that such dogmatic strength saved many ecumenical encounters from banality. Visser't Hooft has always respected Karl Barth, and has defended the essential theses of Neo-Orthodoxy. In the context of the ecumenical movement, such a strong position on the part of the General Secretary of the Council might appear detrimental to the on-going progress of a free theological discussion. Visser't Hooft speaks, however, not out of arrogance but rather from his total commitment to God's sovereignty. He wishes to be considered as a Christian, serving his Master, rather than a theologian representing a school. God must come first. It is no surprise, therefore, to the reader of Visser't Hooft to discover that his thought has been very consistent since his first writings in 1928. It seems that his first vision has never faded. From the Student World to The Ecumenical Review the core of his Christocentric message and the characteristics of his language remain the same.

The published work of Visser't Hooft is very extensive and not yet complete. The presentation of his thought, therefore, must necessarily rest on a selective documentation. Trying to be exhaustive would serve no purpose since he is still active in writing and publishing.

A man of creative mind, deep feelings and great learning, Visser't Hooft never claimed to be an academic theologian.[5] Interested in man, he has always wanted theology to be 'serviceable'. Addressing itself to the whole problem of man's encounter with God, theology must have a bearing upon human dilemmas. Visser't Hooft never retreats from worldly struggles; he never seeks refuge in the stronghold of scholastic theology. The world of man is the _locus_ of his theological reflection; hence, the encyclopedic range of his thoughts and the pragmatic, lucid selection of the relevant points of a given situation. And yet Visser't Hooft never yields to the temptation of theological, ecclesiastical or political relativism. Christ remains the central reality of his teaching. It is in confessing the name of Christ that the Church is enabled to face its own insufficiency. Acknowledging the Kingship of Christ is the _conditio sine qua non_ to the renewal of the Christian Community. The rediscovery of the work of Christ leads the Church to a new appraisal of its mission and of its relationship to the world. Its existence is grasped anew in the reality of the Covenant of Grace and Reconciliation. Now the Church can be the Church, the new people of God, confessing the Lordship of Christ, fulfilling His Will, united to Him in a fellowship of love and service.

It has always been Visser't Hooft's conviction that the Church will find its unity only in the experience of renewal. Although _The Renewal of the Church_ was not published until 1956, I shall attempt to show that the theme of renewal constitutes a _leitmotif_ for his work.

In October 1955, Visser't Hooft was invited to give the Dale Lectures at Mansfield College in Oxford. He chose to speak on renewal, using some material prepared in 1952 for a series of lectures given in Buenos Aires. His choice was influenced by three facts. First, the ecumenical dialogue since the Second World War had centered around the need for Church renewal. Only a transformed Church could be true to God, to itself and to man, and fulfill its task in the world. Second, Visser't Hooft noticed that there had been very little reflection on the nature of the renewal the Church was seeking. Practically no helpful literature on that subject was available. Third, he was further aware of many misleading conceptions of the idea of renewal, such as innovation, adaptation, restoration, reformation--to name only a few. The purpose of his Dale Lectures was to reaffirm that the renewal of the historical Church is possible only in the power, or grace, of the dynamic reality of the 'new age' inaugurated by the coming of Christ. It is my personal view that this eschatological dimension has always underlain Visser't Hooft's reflection on the nature of the Church and the relevance of its mission.

This study--originally my doctoral thesis, defended at the Hartford Seminary Foundation in 1969--is presented in five chapters. The introductory chapter presents Visser't Hooft's thought on the need for renewal. He suggests that the historical Church has failed to be the Church of Christ, to obey the only power which can offer man true freedom.

With the second chapter, we enter into the discussion of Visser't Hooft's concept of renewal. Renewal is essentially a movement towards Christocentricity.

The third chapter deals with Visser't Hooft's understanding of the way of renewal. To be renewed, the Church must be constantly confronted with its Lord, recalled to obedience, re-orientated towards the new age, and reconsecrated to its threefold calling.

The fourth chapter shows how Visser't Hooft relates renewal to unity and rediscovers the Church as an ecumenical society. Newness, like unity, is rooted in the new age. The fourth chapter deals also with Visser't Hooft's understanding of two corollary problems: the relation of unity with liberty and pluralism.

The fifth chapter deals with the concept of wholeness. According to Visser't Hooft, the Ecumenical Movement bears witness to the truth that God, in spite of our divisions, sees His Church as a whole. Wholeness is essentially a matter of choice for or against God whom we meet in Jesus Christ.

I have undertaken this work with the strong conviction that Visser't Hooft had more influence than any other man on the formative years of The World Council of Churches and that he will receive even greater attention in the future as historians and theologians begin to examine the full dimension of his endeavor and the depth of his thought.

Geneva College, Lent 1974.

CHAPTER I

THE NEED FOR RENEWAL

Christianity as its own Adversary

In this chapter, we shall attempt to do three things. First, we shall see how Visser't Hooft links the decline of Christianity with the reluctance of the Church to see its relationship to Christ and to the world in the light of an absolute dependence upon God. Second, we shall indicate how, according to Visser't Hooft, the Church historically has yielded to the temptation of substituting the sovereignty of man for the sovereignty of God. And third, we shall take note of Visser't Hooft's suggestion that the Church, to be renewed, must resolve to live by the Word of God alone, and for the proclamation of the Gospel.

The Decline of Christianity

A study of the history of the Church reveals the weakness of a human institution. Historically, the Church attempted two things; first, to dominate the world in the name of God, and second, to integrate itself to the world. It was the failure of the first movement which accelerated the second.

On several occasions Visser't Hooft noticed the deplorable consequences of this development. The voice of an "integrated" church is nothing but an echo of the voices of the world, its face only a mirror of what the world can offer, a cause of confusion, a misrepresentation of truth and reality.[1] In an essay written in 1938, Visser't Hooft traces the cause of the twofold movement toward domination and integration to the failure of the

Church to confess that: "God and 'religion', the kingdom of God and the status quo, the gospel and the world of Christian forms do not belong together."[2]

His argument implies that the Church has periodically in the course of history yielded to the temptation of identifying itself with its Master in an act of self-deification. Sometimes with pride, but more often with the desire to serve mankind, it has claimed the right as well as the duty to define the truth, to judge human conduct, and to determine moral right and wrong. Such a claim is unacceptable today because modern man, living in a mature and sophisticated society, expresses his concern for independence in terms of individualism. The *esprit critique* motivates his whole life, affecting his religious experience. According to Visser't Hooft, in a Christian community divided by theology and ecclesiology, this new critical individualism adds a further divisive element and prevents the churches from speaking with a common voice to the world on pressing issues; and from commanding the obedience of the faithful. The appeal to a common faith can no longer be the source and support of concerted action. Within a given religious group, points of view on all issues, political, social, economic, vary so radically as to render the Church vulnerable to a judgment of incompetence in these matters. As executive of the World Student Christian Federation, Visser't Hooft was preoccupied with this problem.

Writing in 1931 about the Federation's commitment to study the implications of Christian truth for the modern world, he remarks: "Standing at one of the important sectors of the front we cannot fail to see that the Christian cause is under fire. Nor can we escape the fact that our response to the challenge of the modern world is immensely weakened by the absence of a clear common message and by our easy acquiescence in our disunity."[3]

Historians are baffled by the multiplicity and the complexity of the historical factors which contribute to the modern malaise of society. Theologians are no longer able to reinterpret a Christian faith encumbered with an outdated philosophical apparatus. Christian morality has entered in the twilight zone prophesied by Nietzsche and new morality has emerged from the cult of many new gods such as the autonomous ego, the inherent sacredness of life, of the class or the nation. Writing in the context of the rise of Facism and National Socialism in Europe, Visser't Hooft asks the question whether Christians should not write a 'polite epilogue' to a dying Christian morality. "Friedrich Nietzsche was the forerunner of a great host of authors and teachers who have prophesied this twilight of Christian morality. And he knew why he said it. As he witnessed Christian faith breaking down, he drew the natural conclusion that the time of breakdown of Christian living could not be far off. [...] we have now passed into a further stage and it is fast becoming typical for the present generation to refuse its allegiance to any moral system."[4] Visser't Hooft notes that Christians in the past have had their responsibility in changing morals and the 'isms' which supported them; but they have not renounced morality itself. We may well face, however, the task of redefining Christian morality for "it may be that the particular standards and norms in which Christianity has expressed itself are becoming a matter of the past. Why not? They have no claim to eternal value. Christianity does not stand nor fall with a particular code of behavior, but with a particular relation to God which expresses itself in many diverse ways."[5]

Modern man has come to question all religious forms inherited from the past, and to doubt the content of the very word 'religion'. Visser't Hooft notes that long before Karl Marx and materialism, in fact since the Renaissance, men have endeavored to free themselves, sometimes at the price of bitter persecutions, from the burden of supernatural relations and from the concepts which embodied them. Now, in the twentieth century, the very life of man in our modern society, with all its stratifications and interrelations, rests on the principle of autonomy, on an anthropomorphic and secular concept of life. In such an environment Christian forms, emptied of all evangelical content, may and do continue to exist. This perpetuates, however, the pharisaism that Jesus of Nazareth had condemned, before dying its victim. Visser't Hooft emphasizes that the responsibility of changing historical religious forms is related to the question of authenticity. A purely man-centered Christianity is founded on an illusion and faces the danger of becoming the 'opiate' of Karl Marx. Christians who cling to humanistic platitudes are facing the grave danger of becoming the worst adversaries of Christianity. "The truth is that, apart from faith, religion becomes idolatry."[6] Visser't Hooft believes that Christians and unbelievers have a right to criticize that false concept of Christianity. They regard such Christianity in its religious forms, corporate and individualistic, as a religion self-centered and egotistic; it is a <u>recherche</u> <u>asociale</u> of God, concerned with personal salvation and obedience to Jesus Christ. According to the classic formula, so often misunderstood, it is the receiving of Jesus Christ as personal Lord and Saviour. Faith in God and obedience to him are equated with the satisfaction of human desires. The Church seeks either to justify or to cloak a domineering ambition. Historically the Church has yielded to the temptation of hypocrisy: "in our so-called Christian countries during the last centuries men have tried to hold on to Christian morals, Christian conventions and a vague Christian conception of life; at the same time, they have refused their personal allegiance and obedience to the Christian God. Men spoke of God, and atheism was unfashionable; for God was very useful to cover up the fact that men had broken away from the Biblical faith. But in reality civilization lived upon faith in the sovereignty of man."[7] The Church, says Visser't Hooft, has been obsessed by a need for self-glorification. It has yielded to the temptation of auto-deification and integration. Paul Tillich in "The Attack of Diallectical Materialism on Christianity,"[8] claims that the Church has not been sensitive to the political and social consequences of the concept of divine election. He gives two examples, one from the Calvinistic theological tradition and one from the Lutheran, and he writes: "An example of this is considered to be the notion of 'divine blessings' which express themselves in economic success, and which are taken as signs that individuals, peoples or races have been specially chosen by God. This form of religious ideology is particularly strong in Calvinistic countries; but in the Lutheran countries the ideal of dutiful obedience to the authorities renders similar ideological services to the political absolutism and the economic forces upon which absolutism is based. In the past the conception of heavenly and earthly heirarchies has done a very great deal to support feudalism, and at the present time liberal and humanistic ideas are used to cover up the evils of economic exploitation."[9] This leads Visser't Hooft to confess further that the Christian Church has too often forgotten that it does not exist to defend intellectual ideologies and ethical principles belonging to the past, although they may have helped the Christian Community at one time to proclaim its mission to the world, formulate its faith and spell out its discipline. The Church exists rather to obey God in the quest for truth and the meaning of human experience. Time and again the Church has forgotten that it does not continue in existence because of a political or economic system, the condoning of a protecting power, or the undermining of a hostile one. The Church exists simply to call men to obedience to the only power, which, being not of its nature indebted to man, can offer him true freedom.

This weakness gives the theologian a right to criticize the institutional Church[10] and stresses the latter's duty to remain under God's judgment, in obedience to the Word. The Church owes such self-criticism to itself, to God and to the world. The Church not only must examine all that the historical critics say, but even ask them for help in defining the very nature of the dangers it faced in the past and still encounters today. Visser't Hooft underlines two such dangers in contrast with each other and yet closely related: the danger of deification and that of integration.

The Temptations of the Church -- The Periods of Marriage, Tolerance, and Rivalry.

In an article written in 1940, Visser't Hooft claims that in the history of the relations between the Church and Europe we may distinguish three periods which he calls "the period of Marriage," "the period of Tolerance," and "the period of Rivalry."[11] It is impossible to think of the Christian religion and understand its development apart from the world in which it assumes its historical dimension. The corporate and social character of Christianity makes it extremely sensitive to human relations and to the influence of the surrounding secular society. Paul Tillich stresses that all religion at one stage of its development becomes a social phenomenon, conditioned by its very nature. Then he remarks that: "As soon as a religion grows beyond the first stage of being a small sect, a conscious or unconscious process of assimilation takes place by which the Church becomes part of the given social structure with its relationship of power. One cannot blame Christianity or any other religious or philosophical groups for this development. The only question is, how strong the critical forces remain which in the name of the original principles oppose the sociological and political consequences of this growing ecclesiasticism. It is not the assimilation to the social conditions of a given epoch, but the lack of prophetic protest against the basis for a justifiable attack upon Christianity. But such an attack is then fundamentally a Christian attack, quite irrespective of whether it comes from inside or the outside."[12] The last part of this statement suggests that certain fundamental questions can no longer be ignored or underestimated by conscientious historians; for example does the Church resist the danger of integration to, and deification of, either the world or its own institutional structures? Can we speak of the corruption of the very concept of Christianity in its historical forms?

Visser't Hooft addresses himself to those questions. He remarks that some churches have tried either to dismiss or to rationalize them. In that connection, he notes the Catholic distinction between the Una Sancta, uncorrupted which need not to be renewed --- the reality of the Church being in Christ--, and the ecclesia peccatorum, or the historical reality open to corruption, which stands constantly in need of renewal, but cannot be renewed unless it be in Christ.

Reflecting upon the significance of the 'People of God', Visser't Hooft suggests that only a questionable identification of the Church with Christ himself will allow the distinction between the Una Sancta and the ecclesia peccatorum: it depends, of course, upon the theological content we give to the concept of the 'Body of Christ', and the kind of relation we discover between the 'Head' and the 'members'. We shall return to this important point in the second chapter of our study. Truly, the institution of the Church of Christ, remains the highest expression of God's relation to man, and of his plan of salvation; it needs not to be renewed. It is also true, however, that the

Church of Christ exists only in the historical dimensions which are those of the incarnation. In that human context, from which it takes its historical being, the Church needs to be renewed, for "the Church is not the Kingdom. It expects the Kingdom and preaches the gospel of the Kingdom. The New Jerusalem is still above."[14] In dealing with the problem of renewal, Visser's Hooft is not interested with an idea of the Church, but with the 'people of God'. What are the essential conditions for the Church to remain the true representative of God's relation to mankind and the world?

This question is most difficult. The historian must clarify his terminology in order to keep the problem of integration and deification in proper prespective and to avoid the criticism of taking sides with a hostile world. The historian, for example, can speak of the 'integration' of the Church to the world, or more simply of its 'compliance' with it, only after a thorough examination of the historical situation. In discussing 'integration', for example, one could deplore the loss of the very essence of the Gospel, whereas in the case of simple 'conformity', one faces only a weakening of the integrity of the institutional Church.

As it has already been suggested, it would be wrong to blame the Church for having answered the call of the various cultures in which it developed. There is proper and indeed inevitable relation between the Gospel and Culture. In fact, Christianity could never have expanded without incorporating into itself certain cultural elements it later transformed and used in the elaboration of new forms. Christianity has been and is still being shaped by the world, and the world by Christianity.[15] Writing on the eve of the 1937 Oxford Conference on Church, Community, and State, Visser't Hooft noted the importance of the 'concrete setting' of the Church. He had this to say: "It is impossible to understand a Church apart from its concrete setting. For a Church is not only what it claims to be according to its doctrine, but also what it actually says and does (and does not say and do) in relation to its environment. To say this is not to deny that the Church is more than a sociological grouping, but to affirm that the Church, like its Master, takes human form, and that we have this treasure in earthen vessels."[16] A cursory glance at Christian history will help to bring the danger of deification of structures into a better focus. The charge has been made against Christianity that from its first stages of growth to the present, it has merely conformed to the civilization in which it developed, so that very little, if anything, has remained of its original content and founding Spirit. This process of conformity to the secular order had dominated the Christian nations and indeed the whole of humanity.

Visser't Hooft believes, however, that history has played

an important part in sorting out the various false Christian bodies, which at one time or another in the past had a claim to authenticity, such as the Church of North Africa and the Nestorian Church in Central Asia and China. Several factors could explain, in the eyes of Visser't Hooft, the disappearance of a church, namely its unreserved alliance with one particular culture, its unwillingness to change and be used by the Spirit, all factors which can lead, and de facto have led to annihilation.[17] Indeed the very history of the Church like that of the Old Israel is that of its rejection of the grace of renewal.

With the incursion of barbarian tribes and the consequent disintegration of the Roman Empire,[18] the Church of the West, in the sixth century, under the authority of the bishop of Rome assumed the responsibility of the res publica, of maintaining law and order and discharging the functions previously performed by the state. The Church became, of necessity a political power, the heir of the empire. As the empire had earlier helped Christianity, if not to achieve unity, at least to develop as a community identified with and somehow subordinated to the State, so the Church of the West endeavoured to rebuild a Christendom more and more dependent upon the See of Peter.

Visser't Hooft points out that at the time of the Charolingian Empire, a stronger and better ordering of society won to the

Church and allegiance of Western Europe, strengthened the quality of Christian living, fostered a deep spiritual renewal, and launched the Church on a new movement of expansion. The whole political structure of Europe was transformed by the concept of the Christian King. The prince, crowned by the pope or his legate in a religious ceremony, pledged to rule as a Christian.[19] The relationship between Church and State during the Gregorian period cannot be defined in terms of balance of power, for the two spheres of authority were hardly distinguishable in the concept of plenitudo potestatis. All human endeavours were permeated by the teaching and ideals set forth by the Gospel. Theology was regarded as the 'Queen of sciences' and became supreme in the university. The papacy served the gigantic effort to christianize the structures of society by acting as guardian of truth, morality, and political balance. In 1940 Visser't Hooft could note still that this medieval pattern had remained the ideal of the Roman Catholic Church. "A discussion of the relations between the Roman Catholic Church and its environment must take the medieval solution of that problem as its starting-point. For the unified culture of the period which found its climax in the thirteenth century remains the classical example of the synthesis between Catholic doctrine and civilization in general. The Church created a social order; but in the process the Church's conception of itself was profoundly modified."[20] Visser't Hooft describes the Middle

Ages as a 'marriage' between the Church and Europe;[21] yet he insists on rejecting the Utopian image of a Christianized civilization on magnificent equilibrium. The term marriage is well chosen in the sense that in moulding Europe, the Church was itself transformed. He writes: "Europe owes its existence to the Church, but that Church in giving birth to Europe ceased to be the true Church. After subduing the world, the Church was itself subdued by the world. A tragedy indeed. For while we see on the one hand the historic necessity of the effort to give a soul and a true unity to Europe, we see on the other that in making that effort the Church ceased to be faithful to the purpose of its Master."[22] Indeed, a decline of the influence of the Church of the West occured at the time of the emergence of the new nations. Their princes aspired to be absolute, and attempted within the borders of their kingdoms to control the Church. France and England are obvious examples of the use of the Christian faith as an instrument of political power and social tranquility. The popes reacted, and in their effort to maintain their supremacy, used the same political methods, thus further corrupting Christianity. The Church, which has reigned with and through the secular prince, became finally his victim. The Great Western Schism was the Church's greatest humiliation.

The Church also succumbed to the Renaissance, with its confidence in man's reason. And yet, as K. S. Latourette remarks,

the Renaissance outwardly conforming or cynical, was a child of
the Church, for "its very emphasis on man was in part an expression of that dignity of the human soul which is one of the basic
convictions inculcated by the Gospel.[23] The Church proved unable, however, to channel that movement. The age of faith was
over; the secularization of Europe had begun.[24] Although Calvin
and Luther were seeking a Church no longer imprisoned in the
immense system of civilization it had built, but free to find
its soul again and to preach the Gospel, the Reformation failed
to achieve this ideal. The protestant doctrine of the priesthood of all believers soon epitomized the process of secularization and a new integration of the Church to the world. Western
Christendom was entering a new cycle,--a new period of 'tolerance'--which produced a paradox of assimilation and estrangement.
Visser't Hooft notes that after the two great revolts against
the identification of the Church and the world--one the
Renaissance, Humanism, and later Rationalism and Liberalism; the
other the Reformation--Europe began to live alongside, but in
indifference to the Church: "The great currents of thought and
of life take small account of the Church. It is the time of
laissez faire, laissez aller, and of tolerance based on general
indifference to things divine, and the Church, which has ceased
to be aggressive, submits to being considered a 'private concern'
and is far too easily content with the small corner kindly left

to it."[25] The principle of cujus regio ejus religio precipitated the movement which ended in some instances in the control of the Church by the State and the emergence in Germany of the Landeskirchen. The ruler of each particular territory assumed the function of Summus Episcopus.

The State soon began to develop absolutist tendencies, and put "the Church in a position very different from that which the Reformers had desired for it. Instead of fulfilling the demands of the Church, it claimed the right to interfere in Church life, and that not only in matters of constitution and discipline, but also in matters of faith and worship. In the eighteenth century it became the current conception among constitutional theorists that the exercise of religion should be not only supervised, but also controlled by the Government."[26] In Gallican France the pope of the Post-Tridentine Church--which had completely misunderstood the Reformation movement[27] was recognized only as a symbol of orthodoxy and unity; his direct jurisdiction upon the national Church was curtailed by the claims of the absolute King.

The theory of the divine right of kings, which had claimed Christian sanction, provided the monarch with a strong argument against the pope. As the Church had been secularized by a political pope, the State was now idolized by the Christian prince.

From the sixteenth to the nineteenth century, orthodoxy itself declined under the attacks of the philosophers, who believed in a deistic God, not a Christian God.[28] The quest for God was equated to the pursuit of one's happiness mainly through the promotion of ethics and of a better ordering of society.[29] In Germany the Aufklarung tended to scepticism and atheism. Later, Kant based his theological system upon the foundation of a moral obligation. God became a concept to be reached by mental exercise, and formulated in terms of rational categories. In France, the Encyclopedia was destructive of the traditional concept of authority. God stood outside the drama of the human condition and human history. The foundation and guarantee of social homogeneity was lost. Visser't Hooft comments: "Society became less and less homogeneous, and more and more secularized, as the waves of the Enlightenment, of the French Revolution, and of Marxist socialism passed over Europe. The intellectual classes became largely indifferent to all religion, or turned to non-Christian philosophies. The working classes lost their confidence in the Church, because it was too closely boundup with the 'capitalist' State, or because it did not show sufficient sympathy with the cause of social justice.[30] A new utilitarian notion of Christianity placed the Churches in a subservient relationship to the State, in a new Period of Tolerance, or 'silence' as Visser't Hooft calls it. The old struggle between the Church, insisting on being autonomous, and the State, regarding the Church as ancillary to its power, had marked the development of

Western Europe, indeed the rest of Christendom, and had marred their history. The same tension continued to affect the modern era of the history of a church now too weak to defend itself. In the Protestant countries, more particularly in those of Lutheran tradition, the secular prince, having sponsored the Reformation movement, tended quite naturally towards 'Erastianism'. "This Erastian doctrine was a caricature of the ideas of the Reformers concerning the duties of the State toward the Church. But the Church was not sufficiently alive to its dangers to resist the claims of the State."[31] During the eighteenth century, in Germany, the territorial system regarded the Church as a state institution; at the same time, in England the 'establishment' had practically given the state the jus in sacra. We saw earlier how in France Roman Catholicism had been traditionally controlled by the King who named the bishops and either have his consent or vetoed the decreed of the Pope. Febronianism in Germany and Josephism in Sustria illustrated the same tendency.

In the political history of Europe, the French Revolution definitely marked the end of an era and the beginning of a new age, in the sense that the Church no longer was and never would be again an integral part of the system.[32] Visser't Hooft claims that the Church failed to read the signs of the time. It failed to be spiritually independent and aggressive. It lived in complete isolation until the middle of the nineteenth century, a period which coincides in France with the liberalism of Félecité Lamennais and the <u>Avenir</u>, and in the Protestant countries with the various revivals. "The Church was slow to realize that the <u>Corpus Christianum</u> ideal had become a fiction, that both State and Society were developing along their own lines without regard for the Church, and that European civilization was slowly disintegrating as the old common convictions lost their power in the community. Instead of asserting its spiritual autonomy, it accepted for a long time the supremacy of the State, and instead of making an aggressive evangelistic effort to win the masses back to Christianity, it lived on the strength of its tradition. Thus it became increasingly isolated and lost touch with the forces which were transforming social and cultural life."[33] The discoveries of natural science presented a new and stronger challenge to Christianity. Would the advance of scientific knowledge bridge the gap between reason and faith at the expense of the latter? The use of scientific and historic-critical methods of study led to a need for a reinterpretation of traditional teaching.

In the Roman Catholic Church, thinkers questioned the philosophical presuppositions of a scholastic system which Leo XIII canonized in his encyclical <u>Aeterni Patris</u> of 1879 in order to protect it against the wind of change.[34] Four years later, in

1883, Providentissimus Deus affirmed the complete inerrancy of the Bible. This was against any effort to apply critical methods to biblical studies.[35] To take such an attitude of self-defense, was a natural move for a Church which had been so much questioned, criticized, challenged, and humiliated during the nineteenth century. The Catholic Church was not being anti-intellectualistic, but rather fearful of contamination by the rationalism of an over-confident Anglo-Saxon liberalism, believing in man's unlimited capacity for understanding truth and also believing that a society identified with the Kingdom of God could be built upon the earth. Visser't Hooft has always been a strong critic of this aspect of American Protestantism. He comments about the consequences of the "Social Creed": "The desire to be in the closest possible touch with the life of society and the nation, and the gradual disappearance of the eschatological emphasis of the older Puritanism, and of the exclusivism of the original 'sect' ideal, have led to a blurring of distinction between the Church and the world. 'The dividing line between Church and Society becomes indistinguishable [...]. As a consequence there has never been a really life-and-death struggle between religion and secularism in America.' Thus the Church has often become so much a part of secular society that it could not effectively challenge it."[36] The Church feared the impact of this new "Social Gospel" or "Christianisme Social." It feared also the mythological movements and political parties which represented themselves as an answer to the need of modern man to rediscover a direction for his life. The Church, therefore, opposed them and entered into what Visser't Hooft calls 'The Period of Rivalry'. These new totalitarian movements forced the Church to leave behind its eighteenth and nineteenth century policy of 'tolerance'. Visser't Hooft writes: "It is inevitable that they should become rivals to every Church that maintains its pretension to speak in the name of a Master to whom was given all power in heaven and earth. There may be temporary arrangements between such movements and certain Churches which give the impression that all goes well. There can be no true peace between them so long as these movements remain totalitarian and so long as the Church continues to be the Church. So man can serve two masters. And a master who is truly master cannot allow his servants to be internally divided in their loyalty. The third period of the relations of the Church and Europe, the third act of the tragedy, shows us then a Europe settling down into a new house in which there is no room for the Church."[37] The history of the Church has now demonstrated the 'grandeur et misère du nouveau peuple'.[38] The People of God has been domesticated. The Church has succumbed to the Spirit of this world, turning its attention to the present instead of preparing the advent of the Kingdom of God, what Visser't Hooft calls 'L'avenir de Dieu'. Hoping to save its life, the Church has lost it. The Church is dead in that sense that it is no longer a 'new people', a "new creation." In Babylon the Church has become Babylonian, so weak its desire to go back to Jerusalem that the People may be reconstituted, renewed, and sanctified. The Church divided and atomized has lost the sense of its authentic historic and cosmic mission; now it is merely a refuge for those who seek individual salvation. Isolated Christians are not the Church. There is nothing left to challenge the world.

The Hope of the Gospel

As early as 1940 Visser't Hooft listened to those who speak of a 'post-Christian world', ignorant of God and ignorant of the Church, or else consciously opposed to one or the other, or both.[39] The Church is now in the position where it must prove to the world that it still exists and has a unique call. The Church can do this only by standing firm before the three temptations Jesus of Nazareth knew in the wilderness. Visser't Hooft calls them: 'The Temptation of Material Needs', 'The Temptation of the Special Place' and 'The Temptation of Compromise'. Man is hungry for meaning and security; and he is expecting salvation from one or another wordly plan of political and economic reconstruction, assuming that man lives by bread alone. The Church must resist these temptations; it must risk unpopularity to remain true to its prophetic mission. "In a world where the masses, in their misery allow themselves to be more and more impressed by systems and political parties which are capable of constructing immense ant-hills where man may be more or less well-fed, but where he will lose sight of the reasons, the true reasons, for life, in such a world the Church must proclaim boldly the message of a life whose abundance is not material. It must not be dazzled by a wholly external efficiency; it must show that it cares for man too much to let him become a slave. The Church does not need to defend ancient systems, it does not stand as the advocate of capitalism against communism or of individualism against the different forms of socialism. But it defends a truth which has played a great part in the history of Europe, and which came to it from the Gospel, that is to say that the destiny of man goes beyond his biological existence, that he is called to the liberty of the children of God and that this freedom must find its expression in this life upon earth."[40] In the search for man's true freedom, the Church must be willing to sacrifice many of the privileges it enjoyed in the past, namely the so-called right to a special place in society, sheltered from the upheavals of history. The way of the cross must be rediscovered, and cannot run parallel to the way of the world. But also for Visser't Hooft, leaving the world to its fate by taking refuge in a supernatural ivory tower would be a deadly sin. It would be a misunderstanding of the Christian hope, which is not out-worldly but has to do with this life. The Christian hope has power to transform our whole attitude to ourselves, to our neighbours, to the world. "It is utterly untrue that the Christian hope means: "pie in the sky." To be sure, the Churches and the Christians have often behaved in such a way that this terrible misunderstanding became almost inevitable. Whenever they have justified slavery or exploitation by pious reminders that there would be compensation in heaven, whenever they turned their backs on their social and political responsibilities in this world in order to enjoy a private, egoistic caricature of the Christian hope--they have in fact amassed evidence for the Marxist thesis that "religion is the opiate of the people."[41] The Church must be concerned with the affairs of the world, right at the center of the mêlée; for the message of eternal salvation touches the whole reality of the human condition. The Church shares in the responsibility of its members to feed the hungry, give drink to the thirsty and visit the prisoners. Action is the decisive criterion of judgement; it looks at the future, it cannot be postponed. The Church does not have endless time. Commenting on the 25th chapter of the Gospel of St. Matthew, Visser't Hooft remarks that the hope of the Gospel: "is exactly the contrary of an opiate: it gives a sense of direction. There is an end. No one is fit for the Kingdom if he looks merely backward. Christian Hope refuses to be imprisoned by the past. It seeks rather to introduce the powers of the coming age, the powers of renewal, into a world that cannot renew itself by its own strength."[42]

Understanding the meaning of solidarity, the Church must find the strength of renouncing all claims to a special place in the world. And yet the Church must remain free to be able to serve, warn, denounce and even judge the world: "The Church must remain free in relation to the world in order to be wholly at its Master's disposition, but that liberty is not without the world but within it. In other words, the Church has not the right to allow Europe to flounder in spiritual anarchy and in idolatry. Its mission is, and remains even at the moment of persecution and when no one will listen, to announce to the peoples that all their efforts to organize their common life on a foundation of absolutes or of political myths, or without foundations are doomed to disaster, and that there can be neither justice nor liberty nor true society where God is consciously denied."[43] It becomes now obvious that the Church must resist the 'Temptation of Compromise'. In too many instances and for too long, the Church has been bound to many systems, and 'isms': capitalism, bourgeoisie, conservatism, liberalism, etc... Visser't Hooft does not hesitate to say that the Church was gravely wrong to accept identity in the past with certain classes and certain powers.[44] Has not the Church because of that attitude contributed, unwillingly perhaps, to the crisis of hope in the world? No-one who knows the life of the Church today would dare say without reservation that it is still today the great source of hope. Indeed the Church itself is deeply affected by a general crisis of hope: "And how could it be otherwise, since the Churches had so largely identified themselves with the hopes of the world. They had often preached the same kind of hope which the present generation came to recognize as an illusion. So when that hope broke down it seemed that the Churches had no specific message of hope left for the world."[45] The Church has been guilty of treachery and idolatry, of worshiping false gods. It must be repeated that:" A Church which does not live by the word of God alone or which does not submit to serving God alone, a Church which therefore would live by its human attachment and serve human ideals, ends in doing poor service to humanity."[46] In the last analysis the only service the Church can give to the world, having confessed its need for renewal, is to proclaim the Gospel. Although Visser't Hooft in "The Church and Europe," spoke primarily of the situation in Europe in 1940, what he said can be given a more universal dimension. The Church announcing the reality of God remains a dynamic force in the world to which it is inevitably related. A renewed Church could very well, after the periods of 'marriage, tolerance, and rivalry', enter now into a fourth epoch of 'authenticity and mutual-respect'. In a time of despair, when men and nations could hear no voice and see no light, Visser't Hooft cherished such a dream. With it we shall close this chapter and introduce the next: "It is possible that if the Church stands firm in this time of trial, God in His patience is preparing for us a fourth epoch, a time when Christendom will be not a mixture of Christianity and the world, but a civilization in which the Church seeks first the Kingdom of God, in which the world at least respects the Church. It is also possible that after the third epoch will come the end of time, that is to say the time of accomplishment. But in the last resort we know nothing. What matters is that the Church is found faithful."[47]

CHAPTER II

THE FOUNDATION OF RENEWAL

The Kingship of Christ

In this second chapter, we enter into the discussion of the concept of renewal. According to Visser't Hooft, renewal is essentially a movement towards Christocentricity. We shall emphasize: first, the necessity of meeting with Jesus Christ; second, the meaning of His humanity; third, the nature of His mission; fourth, the extent of His kingship over the Church and the world.

We have just completed a very brief study of Visser't Hooft's understanding of the complex and difficult relation of the Church to the world in history. Visser't Hooft noted:
a.-the increasing weakness of the authority of the Church,
b.-the paramount authority of the State in the affairs of men;
c.-the concern of man to question both, whenever his liberty to think and act as an individual is in danger of being curtailed. All simplistic solutions to the problem such as the return of the Church to the past, the abrogation of dead structures, the right to dissent, or the rejection of all religious experience as illusory will never help man and society in their quest for meaning and renewal. Life through the Church, however, cannot be accepted as a fact, suggests Visser't Hooft, unless we be willing to assess its existential impact on our present situation. It would be most unrealistic today to take the mission of the Church, its influence, its movement toward unity and even its very existence for granted.[1] In 1958, Visser't Hooft addressing the students of the World Federation insisted upon

the need of shaking the Church out of its complacency: "For the fact is that everywhere in the world there are large masses of people who consider this affirmation, that the place to look for life is the Christian Church, as a preposterous statement. Some of them feel so strongly about it that they want to fight the Church; some of them are only slightly irritated by it; most of them shrug their shoulders and let the Church be. It is quite essential to understand why they take this attitude. It is necessary for the sake of the Church. For how shall we defend it unless we know why it is attacked or neglected. It is necessary for ourselves, for our faith in it is weak and shallow until it has been tested in the confrontation with the world."[2] The concern of the Church for a future life had wrongly become not only the foundation of its hope but also the ligne dominante of its theology and the norm of its ethics. But a great number today agree with the marxist concept that once man has gotten rid of the idea of a future life or accepted an agnostic attitude toward it, he can establish the truth about the nature and expectation of his present life. Man, they claim, should now be free to create a society in which there will be no ignorance, no poverty, no injustice and no war, in which, therefore, the Church will be superfluous. Visser't Hooft observes that "Most of the critics admit that the Church has sometimes performed a constructive role, but they believe that all that belongs to the past, that now that humanity has at last grown up it can do, it should do without this guardian. And the most severe critics, the critical insiders, do not raise the question whether the Church is somehow useful, but whether it is faithful to its fundamental Calling."[3] The Church in fact, is so much aware of having exhausted its usefulness, that, in search of renewal and to maintain its existence, it has now become its own critic. The Church is nothing but a shell of reality, a hindrance to be fought against and destroyed.

Visser't Hooft warns his readers against the temptation of identifying such a concept of man, the world, and society with communism. Since Feuerbach it has been accepted by many outside the Marxist school. "Now we are inclined to identify this completely anthropocentric theory with communism. And it is true that the communists have given it its most aggressive formulation and drawn the full consequences from it. But in a more polite and less consistent way, the basic assumption of this theory that the God-given life which the Church claims to pass on is, in the light of our modern knowledge, just a man-made projection has been advocated in all our countries by many of our leading men and women quite apart from Karl Marx."[4] A more positive criticism of the Church, formulated by all adherents of 'Churchless Christianity', claims that the Church is guilty of obscuring the concept and ideal of the Kingdom of God. The Church has identified the Kingdom with an other worldly dream,

and has refused to read the signs of this time, to enter into
the movement of revolution and change which characterizes this
period of history. The 'Social Gospel' has stigmatized such a
tendency and reacted against its causes. In America the rise
of the Social Gospel was, as Visser't Hooft interpreted it, a
by-product of a liberalizing process aimed primarily at a new
formulation of faith, based upon the conceptions of the immanence of God[5] and of a critical approach to the Bible, and influenced by the humanists and the Enlightment. The idea of the
Kingdom as a terrestrial possibility began to appeal to men's
minds; the rediscovery of the centrality of the Kingdom of God
in Jesus' teaching was now interpreted, by men like Rauschenbush,
as a real ideal for the present world. That ideal would not
come, however, by revolutionary means with the destruction of
the existing social order but with its redemption. If, on the
one hand the champions of the Social Gospel were radical in their
new systematic, and fully developed interpretation of the Kingdom, on the other hand they maintained a rather conservative
approach to the social issue. They could afford that kind of
paradox because of their optimism and complete confidence in a
Kingdom being built upon earth by men of good will, called to
announce and aid the inevitable progress, harmony and peace. According to Visser't Hooft, the First World War shattered this
beautiful dream. Because of its over-optimism, its lack of his-

torical perspective, and its facileness the Social Gospel underestimated the perennial crisis of the human condition and failed to meet the challenge of the day.⁶ The Social Gospel forgot that for the Christian and the Church there is no meaning of history apart from an attempt to understand the meaning of the Cross and suffering. It forgot that in the Western world as Karl Lowith says: "The problem of suffering has been faced in two different ways; by the myth of Prometheus and by the faith in Christ-- the one a rebel, the other a servant. Neither antiquity nor Christianity indulged in the modern illusion that history can be conceived as a progressive evolution which solves the problem of evil by way of elimination."⁷

Visser't Hooft notes that all of the critics of the Church question its usefulness. Many still believe not only that there is life in Christ but also that this life is known, shared and transmitted in and through the Church. What they doubt is the claim of existing churches to the heritage of the apostolic Church. They accuse the Church of living in apostasy, seeking self-glorification rather than service, and triumph rather than sharing in the suffering of its Master. Visser't Hooft does not attempt to dismiss the accusation, but he suggests that the only constructive criticism, perhaps the only possible attack against the Church must be made in the name of God. This is where we find in Visser't Hooft the influence of Neo-Orthodoxy, which seems to have remained always very strong in the development of his thought. For Visser't Hooft, God wills the Church; His design for man is revealed to us in Jesus Christ, in the whole and coherent record of biblical revelation. He further affirms that God's plan can only be carried out in history through a God-given community. We shall come back to this as we study his concept of the People of God. That community is not an end in itself, but must prepare the way for a new humanity, reconciled to God and fully renewed. God, having called the community into existence, has the right to keep it under his judgment and to intervene in its historical development, through his prophets and finally through Jesus Christ, the Good Shepherd who gathers the new people through the shedding of his own blood. This, of course, will lead Visser't Hooft to determine the place of Jesus Christ in a dynamic movement of renewal of the people of God. For Visser't Hooft Jesus Christ is the answer to the problem of renewal. It is only by renewing our faith in Christ, in the power of the Spirit, that we can look forward to the renewal of the Church; this of course is due to the priority of Christ over the Church--a central theme of Neo-Orthodoxy. Visser't Hooft summarizes his thought as follows: "Even though we owe our knowledge of Christ to the Church, we do not believe in Christ because of the Church, but in the Church because of Christ. Our answer is to proclaim that in him there is life, and that he

lives and acts in the Church. We cannot prove that this is not
an illusion. We can only testify that the life found in Christ,
which we received in and through the Church, is more real than
any kind of life we have found elsewhere."[8] The problem of facing the claims of Christ over man, the Church and society remains imperative. That the Church in history has been unfaithful, and that it has often exploited a distorted eschatology to
force men into accepting injustice in this life, is for Visser't
Hooft a poor excuse in escaping the implications of Christ's
Lordship and of the world embracing dimension of his redeeming
work. The 'cosmic plan of salvation' cannot be implemented outside the Church, and its universal outreach. "A churchless
Christ is not the real Christ, a churchless Christ is not the
Christ who communicates life to the world; and a churchless
Christian is in tremendous danger of using Christ for his own
salvation rather than letting himself be used by Christ for his
total work."[9] Christians critical of their community must be
reminded that a movement looking back to the primitive Church
can be very unrealistic and romantic. We cannot deny that the
New Testament Church was also a fellowship of sinners, penetrated
by erroneous doctrines and rent by tensions. Yet, it remained
true to the Christian exercise of the three great cardinal virtues of Faith, Hope and Love, and totally open to the movement
of the Spirit, to the Word of God, and to the judgment of its

Lord. The Church of the New Testament, therefore, was constantly being renewed in Christ; but believing in Christ precisely means faith in that transforming power within the Church, which never ceased to work, heal and confirm the community in its long and difficult history. Visser't Hooft refuses to yield to that kind of Kierkegaardian pessimism or defeatism which has invaded the Church of the twentieth century. Reflecting once again upon history, he has this to say: "Church history is a depressing subject if you study it in the same way as general history. But church history becomes exciting and profoundly encouraging if you study it from the angle of church renewed. In churches in which the Word of God gets a hearing it has happened again and again, and it does happen today, that that Word suddenly proves its explosive power and transforms the whole life of the church and sometimes of the society around it. We can, we must, remain loyal members of our churches because, however antiquated they may look to us, they are the places where the only really new thing happens, the invasion of the new world of God into the old world of men. But that implies that we must be in our churches as watchmen who are constantly on the look out for the first rays of dawn, as loyal opposition if and when the Church does not recognize the new thing that its Lord would do in its midst."[10] We discover already how Visser't Hooft insists upon the 'visibility' of the Church. It belongs to the very nature of the Christian community, which is more than a community of faith in the Spirit. Visser't Hooft claims that there is no life in the simple 'idea' of the Church, but only in the historical hic et nunc of the Church. It is this visible Church which brings the light of the Gospel to the world.

Of the Necessity of Meeting with Jesus Christ

The relevance of the 'here and now' of the Church, and of the authenticity of its mission is acceptable only in the perspective of faith in Jesus Christ, as a present and personal reality much greater than history or theology,[11] whose kingship over the Church and the world is the true via salutis. The Kingship of Christ is in fact Visser't Hooft's most rewarding and best approach to christology, and is his key to a correct understanding of ecclesiology. He has treated the subject on many occasions from 1935, with "The Humanity of Jesus Christ," to his 1957 article on "Jesus Christ the Reconciler."[12] Everywhere Visser't Hooft is concerned with studying Christology not as a philosophical or speculative question but as an historical and concrete question. This explains why his first effort deals with the humanity of Jesus Christ; he did not write his book on The Kingship of Christ[13] until 1947.

Historically the first chapter of this book is most interesting for it reveals both Visser't Hooft's point of departure of source of inspiration and his theological pre-suppositions. He gives us a kind of retrospective assessment of Protestant Christology. Based on the threefold office of Christ, it was a practical doctrine, a genuine example of pastoral teaching. It faced the danger, however, of separating offices which can be only distinguished. Christ as teaching-Prophet, reconciling-Priest and exalted King performs but one work of salvation. Theology has been too prompt to emphasize one of the three offices at the expense of the other two, which is an error according to Visser't Hooft. He writes: "A one-sided emphasis on the prophetic ministry leads inevitably to moralism and rationalism: Christ becomes a great teacher of ideas and principles, but his work, past, present and future, disappears from the horizon. An exclusive emphasis on the priestly function leads to pietism and mysticism: Christ is the lamb of God, but his piercing word and victory over sin and death are not taken seriously. The full concentration of the Kingship of Christ leads to utopiansim and apocalypticism. Christ is the glorious King, but it is forgotten that his victory is the invisible victory of the word and that in this world the road to glory is the way of the Cross."[14] Of course it is quite permissible for theologians, who try to answer the needs of a generation of Christians, to throw light on one particular aspect of the work of Christ; but not on the price of a "derailment of theology"[15] or a neglect of the other aspects. Visser't Hooft suggests that the theological tradition of Protestantism has overstressed the priestly and prophetic ministries of Christ and, by doing so, has obscured his kingly office. Hence the cosmic significance of the history of salvation has been neglected; and the whole world of man is not seen in the light of the victory of Christ. Luther for example wanted to overcome all confusion between the realm of Christ and that of a world created by Roman clericalism; and, says Visser't Hooft, he was as strongly opposed to anabaptist utopianism as he was to papal theocracy. In the process, the togetherness of the two kingdoms under the Lordship of Christ was obscured. This was later exaggerated by some of his followers to the point of excluding the political and social order from the kingly office of Christ.[16] Luther, actually, had always believed in and insisted upon the divine vocation of the secular ruler,[17] but it was a weakness of many in the post-Luther tradition to present the Church as the only <u>Locum</u> of Christ's Kingship.

Calvin, on the other hand, did not hesitate to present Christ as "The Lieutenant of God," ordering the whole creation and presiding to the salvation of the faithful. Visser't Hooft argues, however, that Calvin, in the fundamental passages of <u>The Institutes</u>,[18] conceives the Kingship of Christ primarily in terms of his dominion over the Church. Calvin, he claims, had a theocentric rather than a Christocentric view of the world, although he felt that the civil order should be based on the royal office of Christ. We cannot subscribe completely to that judgment, however, without suggesting that in some clear instances

Calvin's understanding of the Lordship of Christ has a universal dimension. It seems that Christ's dominion over the Church should be regarded precisely as part of and instrumental to a cosmic relationship of power: "to say that he sits at the right hand of the Father is equivalent to calling him the Father's deputy, who has in his possession the whole power of God's dominion. For God mediately, so to speak, wills to rule and protect the Church in Christ's person."[19] Commenting on Philippians 2:9-11 Calvin remarks: "Scripture usually calls Christ 'Lord' because the Father set Christ over us to exercise his dominion through his Son. Although there are many Lordships celebrated in the world (of. I Cor. 8:5), 'for us there is one God, the Father, from whom are all things and we in him, and one Lord, Jesus Christ, through whom are all things and we through him' (ICor. 8:6). [...] Now Christ fulfills the combined duties of King and pastor for the godly who submit willingly and obediently; on the other hand, we hear that he carries a 'rod of iron to break them and dash them all in pieces like a potter's vessel' (Ps. 2:9). We also hear that 'he will execute judgment among the Gentiles, so that he fills the earth with corpses, and strikes down every height that opposes him' (Ps. 110:6). We see today several examples of this fact, but the full proof will appear at the Last Judgment, which may also be properly considered the last act of his reign."[20] With regard to Visser't Hooft's criticism of the Protestant theological tradition, it remains true, however, that Protestantism has been traditionally inclined to spiritualize the Kingship of Christ to the point of denying its historical dimension. The reign of Christ becomes, at least in the pietistic conception, an invisible reality experienced in the souls of those individuals who have been saved out of this corrupted world. Christ had become, in Schleiermacher's theology for example, the inspiration of a community of souls. His third theorem on the offices of Christ affirms that "the Kingly office of Christ consists in the fact that everything which the community of believers requires for its well-being continually proceeds from Him."[21] In other words the Kingdom of Christ becomes essentially a Kingdom or a power of grace. We read in The Christian Faith: "by the power of Christ we can understand only that power which begins with the Kingdom of grace and is essentially included in it. And this itself is a power over the world only in so far as believers are taken out of the midst of the world, and the fellowship of believers or the Kingdom of Christ can increase only as the world (as the antithesis of the Church) decreases, and its members are gradually transformed into members of the Church, so that evil is overcome and the sphere of redemption enlarged. But even this is a power of Christ over the world which proceeds only from the Kingdom of grace, i.e. it exists in virtue of the influence of the command to preach given by Christ and perpetually valid in the Church."[22] For Visser't Hooft this suggests that the Church has no word for the world as such but only for the community of the redeemed. The significance of the Gospel, or the Mighty Acts of God, as history of God's action judging, changing and renewing the whole life of the world is practically denied, or at least negatively understood.[23] Visser't Hooft claims that from Harnack to E. Troeltsch the cosmic significance of Christ has been denied, his message dealing essentially with "God and the soul, the soul and its God"[24] and his Kingdom being the "fellowship of humanity and of love of God."[25]

Hence, de facto, the doctrine of the threefold office, as a historical and cosmic reality, had disappeared at the time Visser't Hooft was studying theology immediately after the First World War. Christ, the Prophet, Priest and King had become a strange unreality. Christology was so vague that ecclesiology itself was for many an empty shell. Visser't Hooft himself has this to say to describe 'that atmosphere of extreme uncertainty': "All roads seemed to be blocked. Orthodoxy and modernism were equally discredited. Christ the Priest and Christ the King seemed to have abdicated. And Christ the Prophet had left us a message which was incomprehensible to modern man and had therefore to be radically modified in order to become applicable to our condition. We wondered whether the Church could live, whether the preachers could witness, if their message was no more than a reference to ideals which did not seem to have any foundation in history and in the realities of the universe."[26] We understand now why Visser't Hooft was willing to follow those men who, aware of the tragic emptiness of the teaching of the Church, were struggling to find a certain way to the true Word of God. Karl Barth appeared to Visser't Hooft's generation as a light in the night, a new hope, and his teaching as the foundation of renewal for the life of the Church. "Barth set out to disentangle the Gospel from the entangling alliances and presented it in its otherness, its strangeness. The Bible became again the Word that had not arisen in the hearts of men, the Word which is not to be handled according to our arbitrary presuppositions, but which speaks with ultimate authority."[27] Renewal begins as soon as man is willing to stand before the living God and when the Church is willing to proclaim the Reign of Christ, the Victorious King. The teaching of the New school was again contrasting the present age and the age to come, time and eternity, the old creature and the new creature. Eschatology returned to its proper place: the very centre of the Gospel, and the condition of man was now understood as a situation of crisis,[28] a confrontation with the judgment of God 'here and now.' Visser't Hooft, however, criticizes Karl Barth's early period, suggesting that it failed to show what bearing God's history could have on human history and how the Christian hope could transform the life of men in this world. He felt that Barth at that time was too abstract, too much "in the air," too much in the centre, between every yes and no[29] to help the

Church find a relevant message to the modern world. A transformation took place in the <u>Church Dogmatics</u> of 1932 in which Barth formulated more specifically what the Church should proclaim to the community of man. It is a movement towards Christocentricity; Christ has overcome the world and is already the King of Kings, whose Kingdom has the whole cosmos for its dominion, the Church for its witness, the Word for its supreme criterion before the conscience of the Church and the believers, and lasting glory for its hope. We may suggest that Visser't Hooft had now a path to follow, with a great sense of hope and joy. This is how he expresses his feelings: "Barth has indeed taught many what hope means. The doors of the prison of historical and psychological determinism were opened. And through them we could see again a glimpse of the other, the eternal world in its dangerous holiness and its awful glory."[30]

Quoting himself in his memoirs, he saw Barth's theology as a key to intellectual and spiritual liberation: "Barth opens for us the wonderful objectivity of God's world. He delivers us from the anxious seeking for religious treasures. His is the theology of spiritual poverty. Many of us who have spent fruitless hours in building up our inner experiences and always found them wanting when we needed them most, have been saved from ourselves, from our old Adam by accepting this great truth that the only thing which matters is God's Holy Spirit and that that Spirit is with those who are hungry and thirsty, not with those who are spiritually well fed. And others who have tried to keep their ideals of human achievement and progress alive in a world where those ideals are constantly submerged by the floods of this unbearably realistic life, have been saved from both their ideals and their disillusions by accepting the truth that God's Kingdom comes at His appointed time and that God relates their efforts to it in His own way, which we do not and need not know."31

The Humanity of Jesus Christ

As we suggested earlier in this chapter we should really begin our analysis of Visser't Hooft's christology, as related to the concept of renewal, with the question of the humanity of Christ, although the Kingship of Christ, to which we shall return presently, remains central in his thought. The chronology of Visser't Hooft's writings is not the only reason for that; it is essentially a matter of defining the very nature and content of the Gospel, which is concerned with a Man, unique, isolated, aware of his uniqueness and strangeness. The reality of Jesus' life is in a sense the Gospel itself; a very special reality because we deal with a very special Being; recognized as such by the disciples and the evangelists.

The first remark of Visser't Hooft, in the article from which we have borrowed the title of this subdivision, is that the meaning of such humanity is not a self-evident truth; for

Jesus of Nazareth was himself indeed a man of faith who believed that the salvation of the whole of humanity depended on him. A man, Jesus differs from the rest of humanity because of: His certitude, His authority, His faith, His entire consecration to the Will of God, His purity of heart, His will to suffer, His claim to be able to pardon with a definite pardon.[32] A member of our race, Jesus Christ comes also from elsewhere; he has been sent; he is the Other. Such humanity is so paradoxical that one can speak of the miracle of Christmas, of Emmanuel, 'God with us;' he is so paradoxical that we should resist the temptation of saying more than is given us to know. The Gospel as a document, suggests Visser't Hooft, is interested not in the human existence of Jesus considered in itself-- psychologically, morally or intellectually--but rather in the human existence set in the plan of God. In other words the significance of that unique existence, more than a compendium of data, is of first importance to the evangelists.[33]

Accepting the fact that nothing human was foreign to Jesus Christ, the Gospel is concerned, however, in focusing the attention of the reader on one central reality; negatively the sinlessness of that human existence, positively Christ's complete obedience to God. "He is a true Man, since He lives like us all in a state where there is the possibility of conflict between human will and the Divine Will. A true Man, also, since He has to seek to know the Will of God, and can know it only by an act of faith, and not by any kind of exterior and objective evidence. A true Man, finally, because that Will leads Him into situations which seem incomprehensible and even unacceptable from the human point of view. But without sin - because He always remains open, prays without ceasing, is constantly turned towards God, gets to know the Will of God and fulfills it."[34] In the exercise of obedience Christ has become the Servant of man, in a gesture of freely accepted humility, rejected by some and misunderstood by all. Obedience led him also to the Cross and to identification with human despair and with sin before he could reach the newness of life he had promised to his disciples. He gave to God all that it is possible to give. He passed through all human distress, right up to the hell of being separated from God. But just in accepting the call to go to the very end in faith and in obedience, He showed Himself to be the new Man. A human being has obeyed - the Kingdom of Heaven is here.[35] By faith the Church discovers, generation after generation, that in obedience, humility and suffering is the only possible confirmation of the truth of the Gospel; it discovers also there the reason for witnessing to the reality of the Kingdom, of the new era in the relations of God and man, of God and the world. Hence, by the character of the humanity of Jesus Christ, the character of his mission and of his Kingship is determined in an act of faith, and in the meaning of such an act, especially in relation to the event of the Resurrection. "He is a King with no credentials but the truth of His Word and His Life. In other words, His humanity reveals what He is to those who open their heart in faith; but it hides His identity from the multitude. He wishes to be accepted only in virtue of His real authority, which is not verifiable from without, but is recognizable to those who can hear the voice of God."[36] For that very reason the same humanity of Jesus Christ is also a scandal to the world, lacking in <u>grandeur</u>; he is a paradox, an '<u>incognitus homo</u>' refusing to impose the truth of his existence upon man, who trusts him as the '<u>incognitus Deus</u>' to the scandal of those who resent that '<u>demi-obscuralite</u>' where we poorly distinguish that God is, asks, gives and reveals. Faith is never free from anxiety or at least uncertainty.[37]

This leads Visser't Hooft to the conclusion that the act of determining the true significance of the humanity of Jesus Christ must have the character of a decision, of a risk, of a personal act bringing with it a measure of certitude, but never security. In that sense faith in Christ is already an act of Hope.

Jesus Christ the Reconciler

Here we do not follow a chronological order in the use of Visser't Hooft's writings. "Jesus Christ the Reconciler" appeared in the <u>Student World</u>, in 1957, ten years after the Princeton Lectures on <u>The Kingship of Christ</u>. But we consider the latter work both as a kind of summit in Visser't Hooft's thought and a synthesis of his christology. Even more important is the fact that we should learn first the message of Christ crucified in order to speak more cogently about eschatology and the Lordship of Jesus Christ.

Speaking of the Meaning of 'reconciliation', Visser't Hooft bases his remark on the important text of II Corinthians 5:17-21, from which he formulates twelve short theses:

1. "Man is estranged from God and from his fellow men."
2. "God takes the initiative in order to bring man back to himself."
3. "Christ bears the whole burden of reconciliation for us."
4. "The Cross is the meeting place of the holiness and the love of God."
5. "The Cross is the decisive event of world history."
6. "The reconciling love of God embraces the whole humanity."
7. "We become participants in God's work of reconciliation by faith and witness."
8. "God uses the lives of the reconciled to make men aware of His offer of reconciliation."
9. "The Church is the reconciled community which manifests the power of reconciliation over all forces which divide men."
10. "In the perspective of the Cross all men are brothers for whom Christ died. That is the basis of our solidarity with all men."

11. "The reconciled can therefore never so take sides in the conflict of human interests and passions that they come to treat any group of men as enemies. They seek rather to build bridges of reconciliation between nations, races, classes, sexes and individuals."

12. "Since God's reconciling love is holy Love, reconciliation never means condoning injustice and evil."[38]

These titles are most interesting in the sense that they give also a compendium of what could be a study on renewal understood as a new relationship of man with God and his fellowmen in society in the light of the Cross of Christ. Perhaps we could suggest that we find here, in a relatively short article, Visser't Hooft at his best; the tone is pastoral and the vision definitely ecumenical. The author looks at the Cross of Christ as an event, the central fact of Christianity upon which all the rest, love and Christian ethics, is built. He calls that central event of the Cross the "factual root" of Christianity.[39] It is the great weakness of the Church today, suggests Visser't Hooft, that it fails to remind this generation that the Cross is the center of world history--the basic claim of the faith. Too often we think of Christianity as nothing but morality. Have we become so moralistic that those who hear us never get a chance to discover that the centre of Christianity is the fact of the Cross of Christ? Paul does not say, 'I came to preach about love in general.' Paul says; "I came to preach the gospel of Christ crucified.'[40] The sinful compromise of the Church is to live as if there were no Cross, says Visser't Hooft;[41] a weakness explained by a reluctance to confess that man is truly estranged from God and from his fellowmen and needs the Cross as a God-given instrument of reconciliation and renewal. Even the Church is tempted to listen to those who think that man's alienation from his fellowmen is due entirely to the bad or evil structures of society, which should be changed by a revolutionary process, as the Marxists have suggested. There are those who believe that man's alienation is due to a psychological mal-adjustment and that by therapeutic means man's behavior could be re-oriented and his estrangement would cease. Indeed, there is a measure of truth in all that; but Visser't Hooft still recognizes the fundamental estrangement of man due to sin, to the misuse of freedom. Rather than accepting freedom in fellowship with God, man preferred a life of freedom away from God, which ultimately meant slavery, isolation and despair. "This happened because he [man] had cut the basic relation, the freedom with which he was free for God."[42] Indeed man would be doomed if it were not for God's initiative to reconcile the world into himself in Jesus Christ, to redeem man from the power of sin.[43] For Visser't Hooft, the meaning of the Cross is not to be found so much in the physical suffering of Christ; other men have suffered physically as much as Christ or even more, as in the spiritual suffering of the

'One for many.' The concept of 'the vicarious suffering' from Isaiah to St. Paul is part of the very texture of biblical revelation; it is essentially related to atonement and expiation as well as to reconciliation. And yet it is a scandal to the modern man who in his egocentricity cannot accept that another man may stand before God in his stead nor believe in a forgiveness so tragic and so costly. Man has lost the sense of the Holiness of God, which incites Visser't Hooft to say that: God's love is never sentimental or cheap love, but a holy love. God cannot, does not, trifle with His own holiness, because then God would cease to be God, then the foundations of His world would shake. Then we would no longer know what is true, what is good. When God reconciles man to Himself, there must be a real recognition of His Holiness. That is why in reconciliation there is included atonement or expiation.[44] In other words man should accept that in the perspective of the Cross reconciliation presupposes the recognition of the holiness of God and the necessity of atonement.

The fact of the Cross is central and it embraces the whole of humanity. The message of reconciliation for Visser't Hooft is "a message with cosmic repercussions."[45] He echoes Barth's The Humanism of God in stressing that God is interested in the total human race, in the sense that Jesus Christ represents the new humanity recreated by his redemptive act. Individuals become participants in this work of reconciliation by faith, by accepting it as the dynamic force of their lives, a force of forgiveness, healing, reparation, and renewal.[46] The Church itself, as a community, must demonstrate this power of reconciliation, as we shall see in the last chapter. Such a demonstration, however, can be possible only in an ecumenical movement. Visser't Hooft is quite explicit on that matter: At this point we can recognize more deeply and clearly the importance of the ecumenical movement. Some people still think that the main raison d'être of the ecumenical movement is cooperation among the churches and the exertion of a good influence in the world. But there is more to it than that. The ecumenical movement exists to manifest the reconciling power of the Cross. If the Church fails to bring Christians of different nations, races and classes deeply together, it misses its opportunity to demonstrate the transforming power of the Cross, and makes it harder for the world to understand what the message of reconciliation is all about.[47]

The Kingship of Christ

Reconciliation is perfected, or is being perfected in the Kingship of Christ, which is the object and core of the faith; Jesus is Lord (Phil. 2:11), and the power of salvation (Rom. 10: 13). Indeed the necessity of confessing the name of the Lord Jesus Christ is absolute, for that Name is above all names; the very destiny of man and of the world has been entrusted to the almighty bearer of that glorious Name. In the oldest form of the Kerugma we find the claim for Christ of the cosmic Lordship announced by the prophets of Israel.[48] The Chosen People had looked forward to the coming of the Messiah (Is. 52-7); Jesus proclaimed that that long period of expectation was ended; "God reigneth," "the Kingdom is at hand" (Mk. 1:15). In his preaching of the Kingdom, Jesus refers both to a coming event and to a present reality, discovered by faith in the midst of the community (Lk. 17:21), manifested by the proclamation of the Gospel. In a very short formulation Visser't Hooft expresses that kind of paradox: "The Kingdom of God is still a matter of the future, because it is only existent in the words and deeds of Jesus. But it is a matter of the present because it is really among us in him."[49] The last sentence underlines the faith of the Church in the identification of Jesus and the Kingdom.[50] In Christ the reality of the Kingdom is manifested to man, but it can be received only by those who can see it in the Spirit; for Christ, contrary to the political and nationalistic dreams of Israel, comes to his people as a hidden King. Here again we find another paradox. Jesus Christ, says Visser't Hooft, "is not a King according to man-made categories."[51] Jesus Christ is a priestly King, whose Kingdom, rooted in God's plan of salvation, reveals itself in a Cross and exercises its authority by no other weapon than the Word of God. The priestly King is also a prophet King.

Since the resurrection and the ascension, Christ the King sits at the right hand of God where he reigns with God until he comes again to judge the world. In the eschatological perspective the Kingdom remains, therefore, a promised and future reality to be revealed at the ultimate hour of history. And yet we are not under the obligation of choosing between a 'futurist' and a 'realized' eschatology,[52] because, according to the Gospel, Jesus, the Lord, has overcome and is now overcoming the world (Mt. 12:29, Lk. 11:20-22). The victory yet to be achieved is already the glory of the King. Visser't Hooft keeps in balance the two aspects or elements of eschatology: "Now it is striking that the New Testament authors do not seem to feel that there is a contradiction between the victory achieved once for all and the victory still to be won. [...] The victory is achieved in so far as the demonic forces are under control. But they still exist and the ultimate victory which will bring their total annihilation is therefore still to be won."[53] The Church exists in the time between victories. To remain alert and open to the movement of the Spirit it must avoid the futurist interpretation of the Kingdom, although it seems very biblical at first. It is negative in that it separates the Church from the world in a 'holier-than thou' attitude, leaving the unredeemed society to the Prince of this world, and distorting the function of the Church in a soul-saving mission. Moreover, such an understanding of the Kingdom deprives the Christian of the hope of 'the new creation'; as such it is unbiblical, for the Prince of the world is already judged (Jn. 12:13, 16:11). 'Realized' eschatology, on the other hand, is equally dangerous for Visser't Hooft, because it can lead to a passive attitude in the face of social evils. It tends to equate the Church and the Kingdom. Everything has happened; there is very little room left, if any, for expectation, hope and humility. The Church has no sense of need, no desire for renewal. This interpretation leads to an optimistic faith in the progressive penetration of the world by the forces of Church and Kingdom. But it cuts the nerve of the Biblical outlook.[54] The tension which keeps the Church alert and obedient is taken away. The whole concept of the Kingdom cannot be described in quantitative terms, suggests Visser't Hooft, nor in terms of development or progress. It is based on the relation of faith to sight; first hidden, the Kingdom is being revealed. In terms of Church renewal the importance of a rightly understood eschatology cannot be exaggerated. It will determine the relations of the Church not only to its Lord, but also to man, society and the state. A misunderstanding of eschatology can be very destructive: "The merely futurist interpretation leads to the undervaluing of the victory which is achieved, and makes Christ a potential rather than a real King. But the interpretation according to which the total victory is already behind us leads to underestimating the reality of the adversaries, to the abandonment of hope and to the truncation of the history of salvation."[55] The weakness of the Social Gospel was precisely that kind of 'truncation'; it was to found its concept of the Kingdom on a false interpretation of eschatology, on a realized hope, on the Diesseitigkeit of Christianity. The terrestrial dimension of the Kingdom was the central thought of the Gospel around which the social thoughts of Jesus were grouped and systematized. Salvation was now equated to the social redemption of the human race on earth; the new creation was the hope of a new human world. The Kingdom had lost its eschatological nature and Jesus his messianic character and mission; he was reduced to a mere social reformer. Visser't Hooft underlines the weakness of the Social Gospel in men like L. Abbott, R. T. Ely and even Rauschenbush, when he says that "the strongest accent is always rather on the teaching than on the saving aspect of His [Jesus'] mission and rather on the example given by His life than on the significance of His death and resurrection."[56] Visser't Hooft stresses again and again that a correct interpretation of the Kingship of Christ is a matter of life and death for the Church; it can be also the most dynamic source of renewal. We must, therefore, try to understand now what is the Lordship of Christ in the Church and then in the world.

Jesus Christ came into the world to fulfill a twofold mission. First he claimed the allegiance of Israel and he died as King of the Jews. Secondly, having been rejected by his nation, he gathered around him the nucleus of a new people, a new ecclesia, a messianic community which would become the heir of the Old Israel and proclaim the good news of the Kingdom.

"'Ecclesia' is nothing less and nothing more than the name of the 'assembly of God' which accepts the King whom God has sent and thus becomes the true embodiment of the people of God."[57] Perhaps we should pause here to reflect upon Visser't Hooft's concept of the People of God in relation to the Kingship of Christ. In 1943, four years before the lectures on the Kingship of Christ which have retained our interest in this chapter, Visser't Hooft wrote a lengthy article on that subject.[58] The inportance of the People of God is neither in its uniqueness nor in its faithfulness, but rather in the fact that it is the subject of God's action in history. Hence the significance of the history of that people is *per se* vertical and not horizontal. It must be read in the light of the revelation of God's plan for the world. Apart from God's interventions in its history that people would have been nothing; with its *raison d'être* Israel owed everything to God. The wish of God to have 'a special people unto Himself' (Deut. 7:7) brought it into existence. The very purpose of that wish and choice was to prepare the way for the coming of God's Kingdom over the whole of His creation. Israel was only a "first born" (Ex. 4:22), an instrument of salvation. He was elected to be a witness to the Holy One. He has failed, however, turned to other gods or yielded to the dream of national messianism. Time and again in its history the people of God has found the burden of election a yoke too heavy, and has rebelled against it, calling upon itself the judgements of the Lord. The sin of the people has been manifold, i.e. in regarding its election as a privilege, or in thinking of itself as eternal, thus settling down in the present, in asking for a terrestrial King, and in shutting itself off from the needs of other nations. God has always been ready, as He remains today towards the Church, to warn and even strike his disobedient people; but he has refused to give up his plan of salvation which still embraces the whole world. His promise remained valid for a faithful remnant, whose relation to God was no longer a matter of flesh and blood but rather of grace.

The message of the remnant and that of a universal salvation has come true and has reached its supreme moment in Jesus Christ. "The progressive shrinking in God's plan"[59] to use Visser't Hooft's expression, became now a "process of concentration."[60] "There comes the supreme moment when the people of God consists of a single Figure. When Jesus Christ climbs towards Golgotha He alone is the people of God. He bears the whole weight of God's work for this world. At that moment there was not even a remnant, but only a Man who obeyed even unto death on the Cross."[61] In that new Man a new people was born and the re-creation of the world began with the Church in an organic relation to it.

One of the main characteristics of the new world is that the traditional separation between Israel and the other peoples has been abolished. The new people, come into existence in and under the One Christ and King, is one and universal, convened from among all the peoples of the earth in the true Church, the heir of ancient Israel. Consequently the Church, the new people, cannot be constituted of isolated Christians; neither can it be equated to any given people or nation. Visser't Hooft in the early thirties, at the very beginning of the national-socialist era in Germany, saw the danger of a national mysticism substituted for Christianity, of a people set into the place of the people of God;[62] in fact he remarks that any form of national messianism will set the people into the place of God himself. The will of God will be subservient to the will, ambition or dream of a people, a nation, a church. The sin of idolatry is a sin of self-election leading to the evil of racial discrimination,[63] and religious intolerance or spiritual tyranny.

For the Church its 'being in Christ' means that it must act as an instrument at the disposal of its Master, proclaiming the promise of a cosmic salvation, working in the place of a servant to the re-creation of the world. It must confess its servanthood and depend upon Christ rather than claim a mystical identification with Him. Christ must remain the King and the Church the handmaid.[64] It is the place where the good news of the Kingdom is proclaimed but it is not the Kingdom. As Visser't Hooft says, the Church is an "eschatological fact,"[65] existing between the time of reconciliation and that of fulfillment; it is a company of pilgrims. Visser't Hooft denounces in Roman Catholic ecclesiology a blurring of the frontier between the Church and the Kingdom.[66] It is a great danger for a Church to lose the dimension of the 'not yet', with its promise of renewal, of the reality still hidden, of the substance of faith, so to speak. For the Church knows its King by faith only; it may not act as if it knew him by sight. The dimension of the 'already' has no finality. "For a Church which does not know that the Kingdom is its promise and its vis a vis becomes a Church in monologue. It is so at one with its Lord that it confuses its own voice with the voice of the Lord. It is so much at home in what it conceives to be the Kingdom that it no longer expects the Kingdom."[67] Such a Church is in danger, therefore, of refusing to be judged and renewed by its Lord, to be re-called, re-formed, and re-created, it becomes the prey of clericalism, taking refuge in its dogmatic system and in its spiritual and moral traditions.

Visser't Hooft suggests that it is only by proclaiming the true Kingship of Christ in the Church that the latter remains under the Lord's judgment, realizes its own sickness and the measure of divine grace, and engages anew in creative action, rendering witness to its King. To speak in the name of the Lord is precisely the function of the Church. Even under constraint, the Church must speak concretely and explicitly. The Church in its very essence is a confessing Church; its confession of Christ as Lord--even at the risk of suffering-- being the ultimate criterion of its life. "Whether a church is on the way to renewal or not depends on its sense of responsibility for the representative message which is uttered in its name from its pulpit." Hence preaching becomes a "speech on behalf of the King."[68] It must be spoken on his behalf to the whole people of God and beyond it to the whole world, bringing about cohesion, unity, and universality. The Church must resist and denounce the individualistic character of a false conception of salvation, and the atomistic conception of society which undermines its creative forces and frustrates its hope of unity. The King of the Church is also the Good Shepherd who takes away the sins of the world and is the Saviour of the world. Christ, the Head of the Church, is also the Head of God's creation. Everything that was made exists in him and through him (Jn. 1:10): "It means that the history of salvation, of which the Church is the main instrument, embraces far more than just the life of the Church. That history deals not only with the fate of individual souls and the destiny of the people of God. God thinks and plans in terms of humanity and of the universe."[69] Indeed for Visser't Hooft the fact of Christ is the centre of all history: because of that, the Church and the world have a great deal in common. The fact that the world did not receive the Light, and is under judgment, does not affect the light itself. The world lives in the light of Christ's victory over sin and death. Basically the difference between the Church and the world is that the former acknowledges the King of the world, the latter rejects him; but "God's plan remains a cosmic plan."[70] He loves the world. The Church, therefore, cannot be indifferent about the life of the world and the worldly powers God uses for his purpose. The function of the Church is to challenge the world to recognize its King, to shift from its allegiance to the Prince of the World toward a redeeming allegiance to Christ. A world which is Christ's concern and battlefield cannot be abandoned to its fate. Visser't Hooft concludes that: "the Gospel is, therefore, equally far away from a Manichean dualism which rejects the world in toto and from an optimistic faith in the gradual penetration of the world by divine forces."[71] It is not the mission of the Church to speak against the world; and yet because it is already acknowledging the Kingship of Christ, the Church cannot adapt the content of the Gospel to the categories of the world. Hence, the tension between the two entities. And yet, the Church must look at the state in the light of the plan of salvation, which is only a part of God's general providence. Visser't Hooft calls for a "Christocentric conception of the state." The rulers of the state are intended to be the servants of the King. The fact that the state in its rebellion idolizes its own authority and, in achieving shadow victories, becomes the 'Beast' and the enemy of God, does not change the very nature of the state and its relationship to the Kingship of Christ. The Church, of course, will have to protest against the misconceptions and abuses of

the state, but it should not refuse its obedience and services in
due times and proper concerns. In the same manner, the Church,
knowing that Christ has overcome the world, should not fight
against it; it should use the only weapon worth its calling,
namely the "joyous and certain affirmation that in spite of all
its Lord reigns."[72] This seems terribly idealistic, romantic
and consequently rather negative. It is the only way, however,
if the Church wants to remain a spiritual instrument in the hands
of God, and live of the Gospel with which it is entrusted.[73]
Visser't Hooft stresses that the priestly-Kingship of Christ
must lead the Church to take the way of the Cross and to intercede
for the world without Phariseeism and moralism. The prophetic-Kingship
of Christ must then lead the same Church to use
the sword of the Spirit, the proclamation and defense of the
Word in order to confront the world with the will of God, never
speaking in its name, but always respecting the distinction
between the Head and the Body. In other words, for Visser't
Hooft Kingship in the Church means "Christocracy but not
ecclesiocracy."[74] It has been one of the capital errors of the
Roman Catholic Church to have blurred that distinction.[75] History
has shown how an assumed Kingship became for the Church a
heavy burden to carry, and for man himself a humiliating yoke.
Christ is the King, and because he reigns we must see the world
and the Church in it as the theater of his action. Establishing
Christ's Kingship is not, after all, the responsibility of the

Church, as Visser't Hooft suggests, the crucial issue for the Church is to live as a servant of the Kingdom in spe and yet already in re, although not fully. That servanthood of the Church should be understood, defined and reformed in the light of the biblical revelation which provides the Church with "the basic insights concerning God's design for man, for society, for the state which we need to arrive at Christian decisions in these realms."[76] The Church, however, must obey the Word with the responsibility of true spiritual freedom, avoiding all forms of biblicism which would absolutize specific historical situations in the Bible. By compelling the New Israel to use the laws once given for the social and political order of the Old Israel, the Church would deny de facto that God's Word is a living Word. In terms of ethics, the Bible does not give any ready-made answers. It is not a manual of casuistry. It only shows the way of obedience to the King. And yet the Church of today needs as much a Biblical social ethics as the Church of the beginning of the century needed a Biblical theology. It will help the Church to understand better a true conception of man in all his relationships, and the true meaning of a social gospel, concerned with the whole life of the whole community, and with the individual man hungry for justice and liberty.

The Church to be renewed must, therefore, turn to Christ the King and to his Gospel. This is a kind of lieu commun; but is it really? Without any hesitation, Visser't Hooft stresses that need and raises that question. The way we understand both will help us to discover the true concept of Church renewal. "The Church whose Lord is Lord of the world need not to look elsewhere for its marching orders. All that it needs is to turn to its King, and to receive again and again his priestly gift of himself and his prophetic word. The great question is whether it has sufficient faith to count on him alone and not to divide its allegiance. If it has, it will find that it is never left without the knowledge of his will and the power to do it."[77]

CHAPTER III

THE WAY OF RENEWAL

The Threefold calling of the Church

In this third chapter we shall see that, according to Visser't Hooft, the message of renewal is part of God's revelation in Jesus Christ. Renewal, therefore, could be neither a human act nor a structural reform. It is an intervention of the Holy Spirit bringing the Church back to its Lord. It is Visser't Hooft's conviction that, to be renewed, the Church must be itself. First, the Church must be 'in Christ'--constantly confronted with its Lord. Second, the Church must be in via--making the manifestation of God in history known to all men. Third, the Church must serve the world under the sign of the Cross. Fourth, the Church must be independent of the world.

Conditions for Renewal

In the preceding chapter we have stressed Visser't Hooft's conception of the relationship of the Church to its King. The Kingship of Christ means the direct rule of God over the Church and the world. A renewed Church must acknowledge that Kingship which is the source of its being, the content of its faith, the object of its mission, and the consummation of its hope. Actually, the Church is defined by its relationship to the Kingdom of God, present in Jesus Christ. In its new life the Church, however, must remain aware of the eschatological dimension of the Kingdom. The 'newness' established by the death of Christ (I Cor. 11:25) is also a 'newness' to come in a Kingdom to be expected in the future (Lk. 22:16). The Church is a new creation; like the

Christian, however, it stands in constant need of renewal. Visser't Hooft emphasizes the paradoxical nature of the new life in Christ. "If we look at the passages which speak about newness of life and renewal we find that some of them speak of the new life as an established fact, some of them speak of it as a task to be accomplished and some of them contain these two perspectives together."[1] The whole life of a renewed Church must be marked by this seeming contradiction of realization and expectation and the tension deriving from it; what Visser't Hooft has called the "already" and the "not yet." The Church lives in the world as in a foreign country where the forces of the "old age" are still active.[2] It is the gathering of a pilgrim-people, living by faith and not by sight, expecting perfection as an ultimate goal to be realized at the parousia.[3] The tension between the two aspects of its life helps the Church to remain in obedience under God's judgment. The Church is in the same situation as the people of the Old Covenant. "Both the old and the new Israel live under the shadow of the judgment and in the sun of the grace of God. Both are called to newness of life."[4] 'Newness of life' begins with a call to repentance and readiness. For Visser't Hooft, the Church is called to live a life of metanoia,[5] willing to let himself be renewed by the Spirit. Renewal is renewal in the Spirit; the new life is the life of the Spirit. The koinonia or fellowship of the Church is the fellowship of the Spirit.[6] The Church is being built and rebuilt by

the same divine action of the indwelling Spirit. The Spirit is
the dynamism of the Church.[7] Visser't Hooft equates the two formula: <u>Ecclesai edificanda quia aedificata</u> and <u>Ecclesia renovanda
quia renovata.</u>[8] God's work is the starting point of true renewal
and it is received by the Church in the hearing anew of the Word.
"We must maintain this simple truth that outside the Word of God
there is in this world no true source of renewal. Here alone a
true dialogue can take place between the Church and its Lord.
Here the Church discovers that it needs renewal and what renewal
means. This 'orientation to the centre' (Cullman) has been and
is the great life-giving force in the Church and this is the true
return to the source. [...] It is in listening to the Word of
God in the Scriptures that the Church discovers again and again
what God's design is and what its own place is in that design. It
is through the Bible and the Bible alone that the Church can and
must recover the eschatological dimension of its own existence,
as a fruit of the new age and will therefore be saved from conforming itself to the world."[9] The central place given by
Visser't Hooft to the Word of God in the experience of renewal has
two corollary implications; first, that renewal begins not with
the decisions of institutional authorities but with an encounter
between God and his people and, secondly, that God having renewed
a broken relationship with his elect, will grant the same grace
again and will be true to his own Word. "This is a very practical truth. For it implies that the renewal of the Church does

not begin with more or less solemn decisions of synods, conferences or committees, but with an encounter between God and men, in which God takes hold of the situation and empowers them to serve as his instruments of renewal. [...] the Lord who has created the Church and given it newness of life rescues it continually from its worldliness. The Church must be renewed, because it has been renewed. We have therefore sure ground for our hope that God will not leave the Church alone in our day and generation."[10] Hope becomes a key word in the vocabulary of the concept of renewal, once the Church has acknowledged God's initiative and found in his Word the very substance of its renewed life. Hope grows out of a dynamic repentance and a total dependence upon God. This means that the Church to be renewed must recover its essential independence from the world. "The recovery of the total independence of the Church is an essential condition of all renewal. The liberation of the Church does not mean that it turns its back upon the world, but that it becomes again wholly dependent upon its Lord."[11]

Renewal in the Life of Israel and of the Church

According to Visser't Hooft this experience of renewal of the chosen People has been verified in the history of God's dealings with Israel.

The Hebrews have always seen the hand of God in the events of their history. It is the history of God's patient dealings with a rebellious people. Israel provoked God in the desert (Heb. 3:16). The people questioned God's faithfulness, and turned away from Him to live in 'adultery' (Hos. 2:4-8). God must punish the faithless wife, but not without promising a new bethrothal. The whole of Jewish history is a continuous series of rebellions, judgments and pardons. Reflecting upon the deuteronomic literature, Visser't Hooft reviews the case as follows: "In the second chapter of the Book--Judges 2:11-23--we have the deuteronomic view of history in a nut-shell. It is a radically theocentric view according to which the history of Israel proceeds in rhythmic cycles. Each generation passes through the same stages. These stages can be described as follows: (1) The starting point is: 'the great works of the Lord that he did for Israel' (2,7); (2) The people forsake the Lord and provoke Him to anger; (3) The Lord delivers them into the hands of their enemies; (4) The people are distressed and cry unto the Lord (see 3,9; 3,15; etc); (5) The Lord delivers the people."[12] The importance of that cyclic story resides not in the response of the people but in God's determination not to allow Israel to forget him. This is actually the purpose of his judgment and forgiveness (Ps. 78). Both are the expression of a divine, patient love, which seeks to restore, not to break a relationship. God makes and keeps the Covenant; only the people is unfaithful. The Covenant, an act of pure grace, could not and would not be denounced. God has the initiative and remains the master of his relationship to Israel. The sin of the people was to regard that Covenant like a bilateral contract, which gave them rights before God. The only right and privilege of Israel was to serve God and obey him. The sin of Israel, says Visser't Hooft was to attempt "... to turn a personal relationship which demands grateful response into an established privilege to which they are entitled. But in this way they cut themselves off from the living God. For the Covenant is not meant as an institution which has an independent existence of its own, but as a relationship of dependence in which there is a permanent conversation between God and the people."[13] Renewal means then the re-establishment of a true relationship. It is the turning away from idolatry and false security. Symbolically the Covenant is renewed by God himself in the return of Israel from exile. The community is renewed by a new confrontation with its Lord. But once again God has the initiative. "The renewal of Israel is the work of God himself. The new departure does not begin with a decision of the leaders to return to religion. It begins with a new encounter with the living God, who does not give up his plan of salvation--Hosea 14, 4--."[14] Renewal then, as we said in the introduction to this chapter, is a call to dependence upon the Lord. Election is not a guarantee, an established right. God's action is never superfluous and Israel's life is never outside the reach of God's judgment. It is the task of the prophets to make that situation absolutely clear (Amos 6:1; Jer. 7:4). Indeed, the people is being renewed as soon as it recognizes that judgment begins at the house of God. When the complacent and idolatrous piety of Israel is broken down, the prophets may announce that God will establish a new covenant with his people. A new definitive offer will be made to man. It will be new in the sense that the Law will become so much part of the life of men that it will cease to be a Law inscribed on stones (Jer. 31). Israel will be renewed by the Spirit of God. In the resurrection of the dry bones (Exek. 37), the prophet looks upon renewal as a total change, a passage from death to life, a new creation of the Spirit. Israel may gather the bones but not give them life: "... the prophet makes it clear that even if the scattered bones are brought together, that is, if all has been done in a human 'organizational' way to renew the life of people, there is still no breath, no life in the people of God, until God's own breath comes upon it. The New Covenant will consist in an outpouring of the Spirit of God. That Spirit can make the driest bones come alive."[15] That new creation has been revealed in Jesus Christ. The Kingdom Jesus announces demands a drastic change, a new order of things, new forms of life (Mk. 2: 21-22). It is an explosive force, a true revolution, a new age, even if ultimate renewal remains an eschatological promise. A new humanity is being inaugurated by the new man Jesus Christ

(Eph. 2:14-15). Those who accept God's revelation in Jesus Christ become successors of Israel, the heirs of the Covenant. The promise is to them. They share with Christ in a new relationship to God. The resurrection is the victory of that newness of life (I Cor. 15), and baptism is the sign of it (Rom. 6:4). It retains, however, as we have shown, an eschatological character. Visser't Hooft says that the Christian "... lives on the frontier of two worlds which are in conflict with each other. But in this dangerous situation he is not life to himself. For Christ is at work in renewing him. According to Ephesians 4:23 this renewal is the same time a constant rejuvenation."[16] This is very important for the life of the Church. Since the new Israel is constantly being renewed by the Spirit, the Church cannot claim to have reached the Kingdom, yet to be fully manifested. The Church, like Israel, can still tempt its Lord. The solemn warnings addressed to the people of the Old Covenant are meant also for the Church. The history of Israel was written down for our instruction (I Cor. 10:11). The Church may count on Christ, not in itself. Visser't Hooft summarizes the similarity between Israel and the Church as follows: "... Both the old and the new Israel live by a promise of God, both are in danger of provoking God, both may fail to enter his 'rest', the sabbath-rest of the Kingdom. The situations are identical except in one crucial respect. The new Israel has a great-priest who, though he is Son of God, is able to sympathize with the weaknesses of the people and therefore to support them in their struggles."[17] Very soon after the apostolic age, however, the Church began to speak in such terms as to obscure the difference between itself and the Kingdom. Visser't Hooft suggests that it is possible to follow the development of the conception of the Church in that direction, from Clement to Augustine.[18] The Church is identified with the New Jerusalem and presented to the faithful as something unprecedented, pre-existent, pure, spiritual, and otherworldly. With a growing anti-Judaism ... "there appears in the early Church a tendency to interpret the formation of the new people of God in such a way that the old people has never been a true people of God."[19] A consequence of the identification of the Church with the Kingdom was that the rule of faith--<u>regula fidei</u>--became more important than discipline--<u>conversatio</u>--for the apostolic age. Certainly the whole life of the Church could progress, but in terms of growth, not of change. Antiquity, not newness, was the criterion of purity of the faith and of the life of the Church.[20] The great weakness of that age was to fail to see that the message of renewal is part of the <u>depositum fidei</u>. The Church must be concerned with its holiness. Faith is source of renewal. The power of the Spirit is not bound. Truth is the great corrective of life. The tragic failure of the Church in history was to neglect those elements of the total Gospel; the mercy of God was to force the Church to listen anew.

As Visser't Hooft viewed it, Christian history bears witness to that divine intervention in the life of the Church; it offers many examples of the urge for reform, of the desire to return to the Lord of the Church and to heed his voice. The Church historian, interested in the study of renewal, is aware of two facts: first, that God does not abandon his rebellious people, as we have already noticed it in dealing with the Old Testament; and second, that the Church 'under the Cross', like Israel under judgment, is more sensitive to God's voice. Visser't Hooft remarks: "It is one of the most impressive aspects of the life of the Church in history that the Churches under pressure or under persecution know so much more about the secret of Christian joy than the churches which live in circumstances of tranquility. [...] The suffering Church which accepts its sufferings as trials to test its faith is the Church which experiences every day how God renews its life."[21] The main attempts at reformation in the course of Church history can be understood from the point of view of renewal. The reform councils of the fifteenth century, the Reformation and the Counter-reformation of the sixteenth century are the best examples. The renewal or revival movements of the modern period illustrate also the point that Visser't Hooft is trying to make. Those examples illustrate a negative aspect of the life of the Church; they remain, however, relevant. The failure of the Conciliar Movement, for instance, did not mean the abandoning of the causa reformationis.[22] Even the Tridentine and post-Tridentine Roman Catholic Church which regarded the very concept of reformation as a dangerous heresy[23] produced theologians, popes and saints concerned with the cleansing of the House of God.[24] The renewal that the Reformation sought was not primarily a reform of the institutional life of the Church.[25] The Reformers thought that the Word of God would create the new forms of a renewed Church. Renewal could be neither a human act nor a structural reform. It had to be an intervention of the Holy Spirit bringing the Church back to its Lord.

Unfortunately the rediscovery of a dynamic biblical concept of the people of God did not stand up for long against the natural tendency toward an independent and egocentric way of life in the Church. Visser't Hooft observes that ..."very soon after the beginning of the Reformation we find in the life of the renewed churches that the old leaven is still or again at work. And there can be no doubt that in the following century the churches of the Reformation were hardly convincing witnesses of the message and life of the new creation within the old creation. Their rationalistic orthodoxy, their lack of evangelistic and missionary zeal, their legalism and their institutional self-assertion were victories of the old upon the new."[26] The sectarian movement was not more successful. Of course all sects believed that there was a need for a renewal of the Church. They understood that reformation could not be a single event in history but a permanent dynamic force in the life of the Christian community.

The principle <u>ecclesia reformanda quia reformata</u> became their <u>motto</u>;[27] and to some extent they prevented a total petrifaction of the Church. And yet the sects failed in their quest for renewal. First in their strong reaction against a false dogmatism they fell into a false subjectivist spiritualism. Visser't Hooft says that the individualistic orientation of sectarian life led to a "weakening of the sense of responsibility for the total Church."[28] The building up of the inner life of the individual was pursued at the expense of the edification of the House of God.

Visser't Hooft limits his study of the movement of 're-creation; in the life of the Church ot those few historical cases which show that in the pursuit of renewal the Church once again is its own worst adversary. Like other institutions the Church, he remarks: "seeks the security of the status quo. And almost imperceptibly it slides back from the open, dynamic life into which the Holy Spirit pours his gifts, to the closed, introverted life of self-perpetuation."[29] When the Church, however, is aware of that inner tendency toward petrifaction, and turns to repentance there is hope for renewal. A renewed Church remains obedient to the Spirit, accepts that God may lead its way, change its structures and recreate its life. A renewed Church is a Servant, constantly adapting itself to the will of its Master. A renewed Church is open to the truth; it accepts God's Word both as a stabilizing and moving force. A renewed Church allows itself to be broken and reformed again by the judgment of God. It is true to say that the history of the Church is a history of reformation. Traditionally, however, it has not been understood as such. Visser't Hooft remarks that scholars have not studied Church history from the point of view of renewal. It is regrettable, because, as explained above, the capacity of the Church for renewal points to the biblical view of God's dealing in history. It shows also how Church history is fundamentally different from secular history. Visser't Hooft says that a good study of renewal in Church history "would demonstrate that there is at the centre of the story of the Church, as there is in the story of Israel, a dynamic which does not fit into the categories of idealistic or materialistic philosophies of history."[30] Visser't Hooft does not suggest of course that the Church historian could prove that the Holy Spirit is at work in the life of the Church. The renewal of the Church will remain always in the perspective of secular history a mystery.[31] But it is the task of the Christian scholar to raise questions, to show that a Church founded upon the Word of God has a "curious 'Jack in the Box' quality,"[32] and the ability, when faithful, to read the signs of the times. Even if that effort were irrelevant to the outsider, it would help the Church to ask itself the question of its authenticity: 'Are we in truth the Church of Jesus Christ?' It is important; because the real danger for the Church is to live in a false security, rejecting God's judgment. The same review of history would also remind the Church that it is not automatically renewed.

"The promise that the gates of hell shall not overcome it is not given to every society which calls itself 'Church'. It is only given to the body which Jesus Christ calls 'my Church'."[33] What is precisely the Church of Jesus Christ; or what are the features of a renewed Church? Church history has done its part to open the way and help us to answer that question now.

The Characteristics of a Renewed Church

The Church is to be in Christ

According to Visser't Hooft the first characteristic of a renewed Church is to be in Christ. The Church has not raison d' être of its own. The Church ceases to be the Church when it seeks to live its own independent life. Indeed, the Church has no such life. It shares in the new life revealed in Jesus Christ; it is part of the new age inaugurated by Jesus Christ, of the new world into which the Kingdom is being ushered: "The Church to be the Church is, therefore, to live always sub specie regni Dei, in the light of the coming Kingdom."[34] The Church must live in the power of the Kingdom and depend on it. It must be open to the guidance of the Spirit and expect God to give it a new word and a new deed that it may continue to announce the Kingdom. The Church cannot survive in a closed universe; it must witness to what Visser't Hooft calls "the mysterious extra dimension of the new creation."[35] That dimension is the means of grace--worship, liturgy, sacraments, preaching, etc., ...--through which the

Church is in continuous conversation with its Lord. A renewed Church lives a "dialogical existence,"[36] "constantly confronted with its Lord, reminded of its first love, recalled to obedience, reoriented towards the new age in which it has its roots, and thus witnessing to the world and to itself that its Lord is a 'living' Lord who does not leave his Church alone."[37] To be in Christ further means for the Church to live as his Body, as a fellowship. In The Pressure of our Common Calling[38] Visser't Hooft remarks that koinonia belongs to the very essence of the Church. The purity of the koinonia is indicative of the authenticity of the Church and decisive in terms of renewal and unity. Without entering into the discussion of a difficult linguistic problem, Visser't Hooft indicates that the word can be translated by fellowship, communion, participation and contribution.[39] Actually all four elements are constitutive of the Church, whose members participate in the act of salvation which God has initiated in history and accomplished in the sending of His Son. Participate implies sharing in suffering and consolation, and communion in the love of the brethren as well as in the reality of Christ's presence within the fellowship. "The Christian Church is then characterized by a spiritual economy in which there are no frontiers, no restrictions on free trade. The gifts of grace are given for the good of all (I Cor. 12:7); they are not capitalized or stored away. The description of the give and take, of the variety working toward harmony, of the mutual interdependence in the body of Christ which we have in I Cor. 12 is (in spite of the fact that the word is not used there) the great charter of koinonia."[40] To realize the koinonia is the responsibility of the Church as well as the very essence of its being. It cannot be achieved, however, at the expense of the truth. The concern for the purity of the Gospel has priority. There has always been a tension between loyalty to the revealed truth and loyalty to the "God-given and Christ-centered fellowship"[41] of the Church. Commenting upon the conflict between the Pauline and Petrine developments of early Christianity,[42] Visser't Hooft stresses that tension. He suggests that Paul had no hesitations to stand with the same courage against the greater authority of Peter and of the Church in Jerusalem when the truth of the Gospel was at stake in the matter of circumcision and obedience to the Jewish Law, and against the danger of fostering a separatist gospel. Independent of the Law, Paul would be, however, a Jew with the Jews in order to maintain the koinonia, for "the oneness of the new people belonged to the content of the gospel, and to contradict that oneness by separate existence would be to deny the gospel itself."[43] In a renewed Church the forces of koinonia must operate in spite of all obstacles to maintaining solidarity and unity around the centre: Jesus Christ. Such forces should initiate and sustain all ecumenical conversations. A perfect koinonia will become a community of worship, love and thought, a true communion, dedicated to the fulfilment of God's purpose in the world.⁴⁴

The Church is 'in via'

According to Visser't Hooft, the Church is under obligation to make the manifestation of God in history known to all men. This was the mission of Israel. Since the days of the Exodus the people of God has been "a party of travellers"⁴⁵ sent on mission to the end of the earth. Likewise the Church was no <u>pied à terre</u> in the world. It is going out on an endless journey. Historically it has been the sin of the Church to settle down, to look for a homeland. "The Church has again and again tried to create a permanent home for itself in the world. It has sought to strike such deep roots in the life of the nations in which it lived that it often became difficult to distinguish between the specific concern of the Church and that of the nation, between the truly Christian and the national tradition. It has often entered into alliances with the state so that the things of Caesar and the things of God became completely mixed up. It has attached itself to the interests of classes and races so that it came to defend partisan interests and concerns instead of the one interest of the Kingdom of God. It has organized itself in institutional forms which are characterized by a desire for permanence. It has made the cathedral rather than the tent its outward expression."⁴⁶

A Church building a permanent city on earth, looking with nostalgia to the medieval Christian civilization stand in need of renewal. A Church trying to create a synthesis of the Christian, the social and the political falls into the pit of secularism and needs to be reformed. The opposite is equally wrong and dangerous. A Church which misunderstands its true strangeness in a non-Christian world and yields to the temptation of withdrawal, becomes self-centered, and forsakes its true freedom. "But that is a temptation, because God has surely not liberated the Church from its all-too-close ties with the world in order to make it self-centered and in order to make it forget the world outside. God has given his Church a new freedom in order that it may go, that is, evangelize, baptize, and teach the nations."[47]

A renewed Church emphasizes its pilgrim character and its dependence upon the power of the Holy Spirit to live and act. The Holy Spirit convinces the Church of its missionary calling, of its responsibility to reach the whole oikumene.[48] The Church must give witness to the universality of the gospel and to the Lordship of Jesus Christ over all men.

Visser't Hooft maintains that true evangelism really means 'going out'. Lukewarm Christians question the right of the Church to go out, to evangelize. They claim that the Church is not worthy of that call. Unconsciously such an attitude is a kind of residue of introverted pietism and of a misunderstood

Calvinistic concept of election. The call to go out to evangelize does not rest on the subjective basis of religious experience. The Church does not evangelize because it has sufficient spiritual wealth to do so, or a greater wealth than other religious traditions. "The Church goes out to the nations not because it knows everything better than the non-Christians, not because it represents a higher civilization, not because it looks down on other religions, but only because it is sent and it denies its calling by staying home.[49]

The Church is sent to proclaim an objective message, to announce the facts and realities of God's mighty acts in history.[50] In his "Notes on Student Evangelism Old and New,"[51] Visser't Hooft reminds us that: "Evangelism is not bringing oneself, not 'sharing' of experiences but always pointing to something or rather to someone else. It does not rivet attention on the evangelist but on the good tidings and the Person from whom the good tidings come. [...] Evangelism is then the bringing of the Gospel, the good tidings of God's existence, of His concern for man, of His coming into the world to men who have not yet heard it!"[52]

In other words, evangelism is actual and factual in character. The Church has received a mandate and a message to pass on. That message is not true because the Church is worthy and it is not false because the Church is unworthy. It is true because it is God's Word. The Church must make it abundantly clear that its message is the Word of God who has revealed himself in Christ. Visser't Hooft remarks that in the face of new absolutisms and new forms of idolatry,[53] the Church must not hesitate to speak dramatically in the name of God.

The obedience of the Church is tested by its missionary witness to the world. Indeed, the Church is tested in many ways, but the decisive test of its faith and the final judgment of its life are dependent upon its readiness to proclaim that Christ is the Lord (Mt. 10: 32-33). The faithful Church cannot hold its tongue. Visser't Hooft suggests that it is only in the missionary situation that the Church meets the challenge of its faith in the "happenedness" of God's act of salvation in Jesus Christ: "Now whether the Church believes fully in this happenedness will become manifest in its missionary witness. A Church which is not deeply penetrated by the faith that the crucial centre of all human history is what God has done, in and through Christ, will hardly undertake a sustained missionary effort and its witness will never have the toughness and resiliency, the patience and endurance without which missions cannot accomplish their task. It is only those who offer real news about divine deeds who will stand the test in the day of trouble."[54]

In the missionary situation the Church must confess the universality of the Gospel, which cannot be imprisoned in any human form, in any "culturally conditioned brand of Christianity."[55]

In fact, all churches which face this missionary challenge rediscover the way to unity. "Churches which accept the missionary mandate are brought back to those central objective realities of the faith which constitute the common witness of the whole Christian Church."[56]

The essential truths of the faith become more important than the issues of ecclesiastical particularisms. The magnalia Dei[57] are put back at the centre of the life of the Church. Oneness is found in Christ. The unity of the new community is no longer an ideal belonging to the bene esse of the Church but rather, it is a reality; or at least it is regarded as essential and necessary. "...when churches become permeated with a sense of missionary vocation, they must come to see that unity is the 'esse' of the Church.[58]

A renewed Church, really going out into the world, will speak and act in indissoluble unity. Its witness to be effective, however, must be related to the realities of a concrete situation, of the world of today. The Church cannot afford to talk in the air. Going into the world around also means sharing in the struggles of humanity for a truly human existence. At that point, however, the calling to go becomes the calling to do."[59]

The Church is to serve men

Visser't Hooft affirms that the Church is not greater than its Master, who came into the world not to be served but to serve

(Jn. 13: 1-20). The raison d'être of the Church is to serve,[60] to do unto man as God in Christ has done. For the Church to be in Christ is to be involved in the divine enterprise of salvation, in the service of Christ to all men. The Church must be available to man and society, interested in the problems related to social structures. The Church has been accused of having remained aloof, especially during the nineteenth century, from the realities of man's struggles for justice in society. According to Marxist critics the Church yielded to the temptation of eigengesetzlichkeit,[61] of isolation and indifference. A renewed Church regards itself as a responsible society concerned for the social and political structures which shape the life of man. If the Church today is on its way to renewal, it has happened because we have learned to listen to our critics. Visser't Hooft recognizes that as a fact: "At this point--let us say it openly--we have learned quite a bit from Marxism. We will never accept the doctrine that the economic forces are the decisive forces in human history, and we will never believe that any structure of society can solve the fundamental problems of human life, but we must accept the truth--which we could also have learned from the realism of the Bible--that man is man in society, that injustice, poverty, hunger, can become great obstacles to the living of the responsible life which man under God must live, and that the Church must be therefore not only concerned with individuals but with society as much."

The Church is man's keeper. There is no room for <u>laissez-faire</u> in the Christian community. There is no room either for compromise. The Church should not act as a simple "religious appendix to the state or nation."[63] Because it is called to go to all men, the Church cannot let itself be forced into any political camp. It must act as a bridge between opposite groups and maintain at all costs the ties of fellowship within the whole Christian family. This does not mean that the Church subscribes to political relativism; it means that for Visser't Hooft: "Christians must remain aware at all times that the political issues are not the final issues, and that even the most fanatic and dangerous political opponent is a brother for whom Christ died and with whom we must, therefore, seek that personal relationship which allows us to bring him the news of what Christ has done for him."[64]

In other words, the first duty of the Church in fulfilling its social responsibility is to recognize Jesus Christ in every man to serve him (Mt. 25:40). And yet the Church will not serve man as he would like to be served. The service the Church renders in the world should not be detached from the service it renders to God. Hence the inevitable conflicts, the constant tension. The service of the Church bears always the sign of the Cross. The Church does not decide how men should be served. Its service is qualified by the service of Christ and by the complete revolution of the new age he has inaugurated. In giving his life on the cross, Jesus has entered into the life and suffering of humanity and has undertaken a service of solidarity in which the Church must share. Visser't Hooft regards the death of Christ on the Cross as "the act of unlimited solidarity which must be the point of orientation for all Christian diakonia."[65] The service of the Church in the world cannot be merely a work of philanthropy but a total participation in man's suffering and need. It has always the nature of a real sacrifice. For Visser't Hooft, "diakonia does not need any other justification than that which it has in the life and the death of Christ."[66] It should be truly disinterested. Men are worthy of service because Christ suffered and died for them. The service of the Church cannot be per se an instrument of missionary expansion. It is simply the expression of God's concern for man as man, not as a potential member of the Church; and yet the proclamation of the Word and the true diakonia belong together even when the Church is denied the opportunity either to speak or to act. Man's need comes first, however. When he refuses to listen to the Gospel, he remains a creature of God, a brother in humanity of Christ, the Savior. Hence the diakonia of the Church has a twofold meaning: "... a meaning in itself and a meaning as the preparing of the way for the gospel. We do not, then, serve simply in order to win souls. We serve because we are followers of the great Servant. But we know that the supreme service consists in bringing people to the Servant Himself."[67]

Since the Stockholm Conference of 1925 the churches have reaffirmed that true koinonia must be understood in terms of the implications of the gospel of justice and love. True Christianity seeks justice, corrects oppression, defends the fatherless and pleads for the widow (Is. 1:17). It speaks concretely on social affairs, and seeks to serve the total needs of mankind. Christianity cannot be merely a 'spiritual aroma type of religion' in a world torn between a destructive revolution of despair and a constructive revolution of hope. Visser't Hooft writes: "A genuine Christianity is the opposite of a spiritual aroma; it is an explosive, revolutionary force. It proclaims that a so-called order in which some have all and more than they need and others live in want cannot and must not be tolerated because God Himself does not tolerate it. He wants his creatures to live, not to die; to realize the gifts with which they have been endowed, not to wither away. This divine revolution must begin in man himself. For a change in the outward structure of society has little meaning if men remain exactly as before. But it must certainly also find expression in radical changes in the social and economic structures."[68]

Christian love is more than a matter of language; it is a thing of power and action, a creative force. The Gospel must be proclaimed not only in word but in deed. The Gospel is a service commissioned to the Church by Christ, the Servant.

The Church is to be Independent of the World

Even as a servant of man the Church, according to Visser't Hooft, is definitely an otherwordly Church. This rightly seems paradoxical. It means that a renewed Church is aware of its relationship to the Kingdom. The Church belongs to the new world, is part of a new age. For Visser't Hooft, the otherworldliness of the Church has nothing to do with egotistic spiritualism or with the false concept of individualistic salvation. The Church is not a refuge for saved souls, but rather the herald of the good news of a cosmic new creation in Christ. It is, however, separated from the world by the very nature of its mission which is "...to witness in word and deed to the new creation within the life of the old creation."[69]

Although millions of men may deny it--perhaps with good reasons--the Church is "The representative of radical renewal in an old world."[70] It is the bearer of the promises of God, and earthen vessel of grace, a tool of salvation. Often in history, the Church denied its <u>raison d'être</u>, and allowed itself to be imprisoned by the world. But it is the hope of the Church that it can be liberated and renewed by the Holy Spirit, precisely because it is not of the world. "When the Church realizes again that it is the creation of the Holy Spirit, that it lives 'by every word that proceeds from the mouth of God' (Mat. 4:4) and that 'the Word of God is not fettered' (II Tim. 2:9) the great process of liberation sets in and the Church which had seemed to become a mere reflection of society, or, as Karl Marx called it, nothing but the 'spiritual aroma of the world', emerges in its true and original character as the witness of the new creation which, instead of conforming itself to the world, demands the transformation of the world."[71]

Visser't Hooft suggests that the Church of today is going through that process of renewal. He believes that adversaries, like Marxism, are in fact working for the renewal of the Church by forcing the Christian communities to depend entirely upon their spiritual resources.[72] In the context of renewal, this spiritual return to the essentials of the faith does not imply a movement towards self-centeredness, institutionalism, and inertia. A Church antagonized by the world rediscovers its freedom in assuming the responsibility of being critical of a historical situation. Reexamining the flow of the Church history in terms of challenge and response, Visser't Hooft has this to say: "When the Church is challenged, it can react in different ways. First, it can refuse to respond, withdrawing into a shell, protecting its interests, and attempting to maintain its own life under the status quo. Some churches, particularly those involved in a dry scholasticism, refuse to respond even in the present critical situations in the world. Second, churches may respond uncritically. That is to say that they may respond so naively to the

challenge of a particular situation that they lose their deep
Christian and biblical substance, being betrayed by the current
winds of doctrine. Third, the church may respond critically, in
which case it responds to a given situation not by protecting itself not by adjusting itself, but by speaking effectively to the
world in that situation. To do so, it has to distinguish between
that which in the challenge it must take up and that which it
must reject."[73]

Only a Church at peace with the world becomes over-institutionalized. The sin of a wordly Church is to put survival of the
institution above the consideration of obedience to its Lord.
That Church is obsessed with the human side of its life and imprisoned in it. Visser't Hooft claims that institutionalism is
the main obstacle to renewal; but he also remarks that today "the
Holy Spirit works mightily to save the churches from this selfinflicted imprisonment and breaks through the hardened institutionalized forms."[74]

The Holy Spirit calls the Church away from self-centeredness
and faces it with the challenge of its mission to the world. The
Spirit also may use sympathetic outsiders. They seek the renewal
of the Church in its wholeness but are forced sometimes to work
outside the institution rather than within. Visser't Hooft remarks that the missionary movement of the nineteenth century and
the beginning of the ecumenical movement were the concern of such

Christians who dared to assume the prophetic ministry of the Church.[75] Through them the Church rediscovered that its authority resides in its being sent by God. Its office has an eschatological perspective. It speaks not to give good advice but to proclaim the eternal truth. The prophetic message of the renewed Church is always forward-looking; it is the word of a "watchman or guardian in society."[76] Although a very imperfect instrument, the Church, being constantly renewed, is used by God for his purpose of salvation.

CHAPTER IV

RENEWAL AND UNITY

The Church as an Ecumenical Society

In this chapter we shall see how Visser't Hooft relates renewal and unity. We shall examine first the negative aspects of the problem, underlining the existing conflict of ecclesiologies. Then, we shall analyse the meaning of unity with its two corollary issues: the relation of unity with liberty and pluralism. Finally, we shall attempt to define Visser't Hooft's concept of the Church as an ecumenical society.

The Problem

The essential relation between renewal and unity is not obvious; in fact history, as understood by Visser't Hooft, seems to point to a real conflict of the two concepts. A sectarian understanding of the nature of the Church may put the emphasis on the note of integrity, as characteristic of the true Sancta Ecclesia. Holiness becomes then all important and must be maintained even at the price of breaking away from structures which can no longer be renewed. On the other hand a catholic understanding of the Church may look upon unity as part of the 'given' and regard the concept of renewal as a threat to the Una Ecclesia. In other words, history shows the difficulty of the Church to reconcile the two viewpoints, 'Una' and 'Sancta', in a comprehensive concept of the church: the 'Una Sancta Ecclesia'. Visser't Hooft writes: "From the days of the Montanists, when Tertullian entered into conflict with the established hierarchy, till our own days, when groups break away from the historic churches to form sects exemplifying the new life of the spirit, the conflict has gone on in an almost monotonous fashion."[1]

Enduring fanaticism has traditionally aggravated the conflict. Sectarian primitivists and Roman integralists have been blind to the total Gospel of Jesus Christ.

In its effort to reconcile those two extremes, the Ecumenical Movement stresses that there is no newness of life without unity and no unity without renewal. The Church, like the people of God in the Old Testament, can be gathered together only in a movement of return to its Lord (Deut. 30: 2-3). In the New Testament unity is known in the glory and newness of life which are in Jesus Christ. Unity and renewal are created by the Holy Spirit (Jn. 17: 22-23); (Eph. 4:3); (Rom. 12). We have seen in the preceeding chapter that renewal belongs to the _esse_ of the Church and not simply its _bene esse_. This is true also of unity. Both notes are intrinsic qualities of the Church, inter-related and interdependent. We can see, says Visser't Hooft "that renewal is to participate in the life of the new community, which finds its unity in Christ, and that the unity of that community is unity in the newness of Life which Christ incarnates and communicates to those who believe in him."[2]

We have seen that renewal, the work of God in the history of the Church, is more than a historical phenomenon. It cannot be understood in terms of change or adaptation of structures; it does not depend upon the enthusiasm, activity, or natural vitality of man. For Visser't Hooft, the criterion of renewal is the Church's willingness to represent on earth the new age inaugurated by Christ. Likewise, unity is a quality of the new age. The origin and dimension of unity are not historical or sociological although Church unity has to be visible since its purpose is to reveal the love of God to the world, and more mysteriously the inner unity of the God-head. We shall analyse in this chapter the concept of unity. Our concern now is to trace the reason for the historical tension between renewal and unity in the life of the Church. Visser't Hooft suggests that the fundamental reason is that Christianity in its development has consciously or unconsciously secularized both notions. "I take secularizing in its liberal meaning of adaptation to this age as opposed to oriented toward the new age. It is our lack of a truly eschatological perspective which makes it so hard to take renewal as seriously as unity and unity as seriously as renewal."[3]

Secularization is the great threat to the Church. History has shown how the Church is unequivocally human. Visser't Hooft notes that the Church is secularized, and fails to be the true Church, whenever the confrontation of God with men and men with God is no longer an event, but only an institution.[4] The centeredness of the Word then becomes displaced by dogma, tradition, and law. Churches become dead appearances of the Church of

Christ; their unity is lost or problematic,[5] and the possibility of renewal is limited to structural and sociological forms. One of the difficulties is that renewal in the biblical sense and renewal on the historical level are two different things, the latter being meant to help the Church to live up to the challenge of the former. The same distinction should be made with regard to unity. For that reason, Visser't Hooft asks the churches to 'desecularize' their thinking about unity: "We must not think of it in merely institutional terms. For institutional unity may be very wordly unity. Like newness, unity is rooted in the new age, in the unity which characterizes the life of the Kingdom."[6]

Another aspect regarding the secularization of the concepts of renewal and unity is reflected in a man-centered understanding of the life of the Church. There are today optimistic or naive Christians perfectly satisfied with the divisions of the Christian Church. They see in diversity a God-given means to answer the particular needs of individuals. Basically the Church belongs to men and "they have a right to fashion it according to their own will and insight."[7] Some activists see in unity a factor of efficiency and common strategy. Unity, for them, is aimed at the healing of ecclesiastical anarchy. The Church is reduced to the dimensions of a human phenomenon. Another dangerous misunderstanding is to see a monolithic Church as the only alternative to a divided Church; authority is maintained at the expense of freedom, and unity at the expense of diversity and partnership. A further misunderstanding of the life of the Church is to assign particular calls to particular churches instead of seeing the oneness of God's work among men. For more than twenty years, Visser't Hooft, as Secretary General of the World Council of Churches, has called the Ecumenical movement to re-affirm that "there is only one mission, as there is one call and one Church," and that "our unity has its irremovable center in the Cross."[8] Unity is the fruit of that unique experience of being in Christ; as such it is a gift as indeed the experience itself. To be in Christ is to be 'at one' with His Body. Hence Church unity is per se spiritual. The crucial question is for the churches to widen their horizons and help us to discover the Church in them and its essential unity. This cannot be done except in complete surrender to God's will. "The unity of the fellowship is not built up from its constituent parts, like a federation of different states. It consists in the sovereignty and redeeming acts of its one Lord. The source of unity is not the consenting movement of men's wills; it is Jesus Christ whose one life flows through the body and subdues the many wills to His.

The crucial question for our movement is whether this will become clear in its life. Will the many wills of the Churches and of their leaders really be subdued to His will, or will they only arrive at a purely human compromise? And will the Churches in and through the Council be able to speak to the world in such a way that His voice, rather than the voice of man, is heard?"[9] There is no matter of greater importance to the ecumenical movement.

The Conflict of Ecclesiologies

According to Visser't Hooft, it is a great problem for a Church to understand itself in relation to the Church Universal and its unity. Since all Churches claim to have their roots in the New Testament, it is clear that "Biblical exegesis becomes a main agent in the ecumenical situation."[10] The New Testament can also be used to prove particular claims and can be turned into a agent of confusion. History has shown how disagreement may lead to anarchy. "The interpretation of the Bible is a historical process, during which times of far reaching agreement are followed by times of disagreement or complete anarchy."[11]

The Protestant Churches which entered the World Council of Churches had inherited from the nineteenth century a conception of the Church which was "individualistic, democratic and atomistic."[12] The function of the Church was understood in sociological and humanitarian terms. Then, in the first decades of our century the Church was re-discovered under the influence of Biblical theology, as a new creation of God, existing where God calls his people together. The universality and catholicity of the Church were emphasized anew. The local Church was seen again as a "miniature of the whole,"[13] and it was also suggested that what is true of the nature of the Church is also true of its unity. The local Church is the Body of Christ and its unity and the unity of the whole. Very early in their ecumenical encounter, the churches could reach a certain agreement on the essential aspects of New Testament ecclesiology. Visser't Hooft states that agreement as follows: "It is seen that the thought of the New Testament is governed by religious, and not by political categories, that the Church is built from above, and not from below, and has its source not in man, but in God."[14]

Visser't Hooft confesses, however, that some basic differences still remain. We have seen in the second and third chapters how the eschatological dimension affects our understanding of the Church, its renewal and unity. The Church belongs to the new age and yet is not free from the old; part of the present, it remains essentially orientated toward the future. It is the beginning of the Kingdom and yet not the Kingdom itself. This conception of eschatology is not, however, commonly accepted by member-churches of the Council. We said that from a 'realized eschatology', implying identification between Christ and the Church, to a 'futurist eschatology', waiting for the promise of the Kingdom, there is room for many interpretations. And Visser't Hooft suggests that the conflict of ecclesiologies is situated here. The nature of the Church is defined in terms of its relationship to the Kingdom and, consequently, to the world. If we identify the Church with the Kingdom, we make of the former an extension of the incarnation. The world itself will eventually become the Kingdom and salvation is regarded as a natural process. On the contrary, if we stress the difference between Church and Kingdom, salvation keeps its transcendent character. Visser't Hooft expresses himself quite clearly on that matter. "If the Church is primarily conceived as being in possession of supernatural life, it will be thought of as an 'extension of the Incarnation', and as a body, the life and tradition of which carry a certain authority within themselves. On the other hand, if the Church is primarily viewed as existing 'between the times', and the fundamental difference between the Church and the Kingdom is strongly underlined, it will be held that the Church remains exclusively dependent on the revelation in the New Testament message as 'over against' its own life. In the same way the two views will lead to different conceptions of the attitude of the Church to the world, for the first view tends to emphasize the continuity between nature and grace and the progressive realization of the Kingdom in the world, while the second tends to emphasize the discontinuity between nature and grace and the transcendent and revolutionary character of the Kingdom."[15]

It must be said, however, that all Christians agree that the Church is human as well as divine; and none would say that it is of the esse of the Church to be the Kingdom of God without qualification.[16]

There are many other unresolved issues concerning the nature of the Church which have a great bearing upon the problem of unity. The crucial issue is to determine the limits of this One Church of Christ which alone can exist. The solution to this problem will bring us closer to Unity. Visser't Hooft in his study of the Roman Catholic and Orthodox ecclesiologies underlines the traditional claim of both churches to be the only true Church. Beyond the Catholic Church and the Orthodox Church there are Christians bound to Christ and His Church by valid baptism; there are also Christian communities and churches. The latter, however, cannot be regarded as the real Church.[17] The relationship of separated Christians to the Church remains very complex in Roman Catholic theology. This relationship is sometimes "elaborated in the form of a distinction between the body and the soul of the Church (the latter being visible only 'to some extent'), or in the form of a distinction between explicit and implicit membership of the Church. The baptized Christian who is of good faith, and who does not consciously and arbitrarily oppose the Church, may 'belong' to the Church."[18]

The attitude of the Orthodox Church is different. Of course, it is the only Church confessed in the Creed. Other churches, however, are recognized as imperfect parts of the One Body of

Christ. The Orthodox Churches are member-churches of the World Council of Churches. Intercourse between Churches should not be prevented by doctrinal differences; although unity can be achieved only on the basis of dogmatic agreement. The criterion of truth is the consciousness of the whole Church, which is infallible although a particular Church may err. The locus of juridical authority is difficult to define since the Orthodox Church, contrary to the Roman Church, has no agency or supreme authority for the interpretation of tradition and does not present to the faithful a closed and detailed theological system. Its concept of catholicity is spiritual rather than ecclesiastical. Visser't Hooft compares the two forms of Catholicity, as follows: "the Catholicism of the Orthodox Church is Catholicism in substance, rather than in form. For it consists in the first place (as its name indicates) in a deep attachment to and faith in the true teaching, the full content of Catholic tradition, and only in the second place in a desire for the realization of a Christian universalism or extensive Catholicity."[19]

The case of the Anglican Communion is even more difficult to present, according to Visser't Hooft, since several conceptions of the Church find expression in that fellowship of Churches. They all agree, however, that the Catholic Church may exist in several branches, but not in nonepiscopal churches. It does not mean that Anglicanism rejects those churches for their lack of catholicity and apostolicity. It has developed, on the contrary, a kind of comprehensive ecclesiology, sometimes alluded to as the <u>via media</u>, in order to become a Bridge-Church, an instrument of unity. Anglicanism keeps the Catholic ideal of the Body of Christ, willed by God and instituted by Christ. It is an organ of the Spirit for the extension of the incarnation in the world. The spiritual significance of the visible Church is preserved in and by a definite, Christ-given order in the Church. It is true to say that episcopacy has become for the Church of England a fifth mark of the true Catholic Church and a cornerstone of real ecumenicity. The importance of Church order is better seen in the larger perspective of the continuity of tradition, and essential characteristic of the Catholic Church. All Anglicans emphasize the identity of their Church with the Church before the Reformation, and with the undivided Church of the early centuries when tradition was defined: "<u>quid ab omnibus, ubicumque semper creditum est.</u>" (Vincent de Lerins).

Anglicanism, however, keeps also the Protestant ideal in its belief that Holy Scripture contains all things necessary to salvation. But this does not imply the rejection of tradition. There is neither identity of Tradition and Scripture nor separation of the two. Nothing contained in true tradition can be contrary to the Scriptures; the relationship between the two, however, is sometimes difficult to comprehend. Visser't Hooft writes: "This view of Tradition is, perhaps, illogical in that it seems to suggest at the same time that the Scriptures by themselves are altogether sufficient, and that they are only sufficient if combined with Tradition. It represents, however, the reality of Anglican faith which has both a great reverence for the authority of the Bible and a strong sense for the spiritual reality of Tradition, as God's way of leading the Church."[20]

In view of the Catholic consciousness of Anglicanism, its biblical understanding of salvation, and its sensitivity to tradition, it is easy to see why it works so eagerly for the realization of full Catholicity. Catholicism has come to mean in Anglican theology Christian comprehensiveness; and Catholicity means reunion of all Christendom into one visible and united body. Visser't Hooft says that the desire for reunion belongs to 'the very essence' of Anglicanism, "to the very structure of its spiritual ecclesiastical life."[21] Writing in 1937, long before Amsterdam and before the coming into existence of the Church of South India; he had this to say: "it is no mere accident that the Anglican Churches are more active than any other Churches in the movement for the reunion of the Christian Churches. Their visible unity is an essential element in their whole conception of the Church, and the conception of the Church is at the same time influenced by the desire for unity. They stand in the centre of a process of conversation and negotiations with Churches as different from each other as the Eastern Orthodox Church and several Protestant Churches. And they are hopeful that out of this process there may emerge some day a world-wide Church which will contain both the Catholic and the Protestant traditions just as today the Anglican Church includes inevitably the Scriptures and the salvation of the individual; as inevitably the order and the sacramental life of the Body of Christ, and the freedom of thought wherewith Christ has made men free."[22]

For those of the Reformed tradition who believe that the true Church is found wherever God's saving grace in Christ is operative, invisible unity has never ceased. Of course, Reformed Churches insist on the objective character of the Church,[23] but they distinguish between its visible and invisible forms.[24] The notes of the visible Church can be recognized in faith, and their continuity depends at every moment upon God's grace. The truth is not a possession of the Church but a gift of God, renewed again and again. Tradition, therefore, does not have the same importance and horizontal continuity of the ecclesiastical structure does not belong to the *esse* of the Church. On the other hand, Church discipline assumes practically the character of an essential note of the nature of the Christian Community.[25] It guarantees the purity and continuity of the true Church. Indeed it is the instrument of constant renewal.[26] The Church's constitution in contrast to discipline is practically regarded as a matter of expediency.[27] This attitude enables some Reformed Churches to be open to Christians and churches who differ from them in their ecclesiology. The profession of the 'true religion' is the basis of unity; but there remains, of course, the problem of defining the 'true religion'. According to Visser't Hooft, this is the major obstacle some Reformed Churches find on their road toward unity. "some Reformed Churches would interpret 'true religion' as the full faith expressed in the historic confessions, while others are ready to interpret these words in an extremely broad manner. The Reformed Churches do not insist on agreement in 'outward rites and ceremonies', but rather in 'the truth and unity of the Catholic faith' (Second Helvetic Confession); but while some go to the extreme of refusing all collaboration with other Churches who do not define the Christian faith in exactly the same manner as they do themselves, others go to the opposite extreme of a latitudinarian attitude in matters of doctrine."[28]

We can appreciate how differences in ecclesiology raise one of the most formidable stumbling-blocks to the historical Churches struggling to find the nature and meaning of their unity. It is Visser't Hooft's conviction that the World Council of Churches can help them most effectively.

The Meaning of Unity

Churches with different ecclesiologies and different conceptions of church unity have been able to join the fellowship of the World Council. Membership does not require the acceptance of a specific doctrine of unity. This is not a sign of theological confusion but rather an attitude of openness to the manifestation of God's will on that essential matter. Hence, we must study Visser't Hooft's concepts of renewal and unity with the clear understanding that he speaks in a personal capacity, not as a representative of the Council. An *a priori* decision of the Council for a particular conception of unity would close the door to a meaningful conversation between the churches; and the Council itself would fail in its mission. "...it is obvious that a Council which promoted one specific type of unity over against other, would in fact close the door to the Churches whose doctrinal presuppositions make it impossible for them to accept that type of unity."[29]

For the same reason we shall see that the Council cannot act as a 'Super-Church'. and it must resist the temptation to facileness and superficiality exercised by some 'ecumeniacs'. Many do not realize the dimension of the problem. Visser't Hooft remarks that: "it is not sufficiently realized that every doctrine of the Church implies a particular conception of church unity and that therefore we are not only faced with the problem of differing ecclesiologies but also with the problem of many and various convictions about the conditions and shape of true unity."[30]

It is not implied here that the attitude of the Council is one of strict neutrality. The World Council of Churches must speak on unity; but it cannot take sides on those problems, concerning the concrete forms of unity, which still divide the churches. It need not be apologetic for clarifying its very raison d'être: "We can only fulfil our principal function if we seek to speak as substantially about church unity as we can, without breaking our promise to our member Churches that they will not be put under any kind of pressure to adopt particular concrete schemes of reunion. Consider what a World Council would be like which merely said that unity is a good thing, but never had anything to say about the nature of unity. It would be characterised by total stagnation."[31]

What is meant is that the authority, or weight, of the Council's utterances on unity depends on the acceptance they receive in the member churches. The Council has the responsibility to take a stand and the Churches have the authority to validate it.[32] The attitude of the World Council of Churches has often been misunderstood. Some have criticized the Council for seeking organic unity as an end in itself at the price of truth. Visser't Hooft affirms very strongly that the Council does not believe in union per se, and rejects doctrinal relativism as a danger of ecumenism. Actually, as we are trying to show it here, the accent is put on renewal: "We think and talk to much about the ecumenical movement as if it were only interested in the unity of the Church. As a matter of fact it has never concentrated exclusively on the reunion of the churches. The unofficial slogan of the Oxford Conference of 1937: 'let the Church be the Church' was in fact an expression of a deep and widespread awareness that the churches stood in need for a radical renewal."[33]

Other critics of the Council have so much confused unity and its manifestation as to infer that the member Churches deny the existence of the true Church of Christ and look to the Una Sancta as a reality yet to come.[34] Visser't Hooft answers that the fact that the member Churches of the Council do not believe that they alone represent the true Church does not mean that they deny the existence of the Church of Christ. This of course can be applied to unity, which exists in am imperfect form: "There is a fundamental difference between the statement that the essential unity of the Church of Christ does not exist and the statement that it is not adequately manifested. The vast majority of the Churches in the World Council of Churches believe precisely that the unity of the Church is a given unity and this means an existing unity."[35]

Since the very beginning the modern ecumenical movement has confessed that the Church is endowed with an indissoluble unity by reason of Christ's self-identification with His people. The fulness of that given unity has not been clearly manifested in history. But if we may speak of the oneness of the Church in

Christ, we must also speak of the oneness of the Church in its earthly pilgrimage. "as a growth from its unity as given to its unity as fully manifested."[36] As they are renewed by the Spirit and seek to understand what the Lord says to them, the Churches discover with greater insight the meaning of their unity in Christ. 'The giveness of unity' and 'the manifestation of unity' are both essential expression in all ecumenical encounter. Unfortunately their relation to each other is blurred by the theologies and ecclesiologies of the various confessional bodies. It is very difficult for the World Council to find a common terminology of ecumenics. Indeed it seems to be at times an impossible task; after fifteen years or more Visser't Hooft's evaluation of the problem remains correct. "In this whole matter we are however faced with the great difficulty that the categories of our theological thought as they grown out of our various confessional backgrounds are inadequate to express what we have found. Our theologies and particularly our ecclesiologies have not caught up with the new ecumenical situation. There are too few theologians who have awoken to the fact that new answers must be given to the new questions which have arisen as a result of our ecumenical encounter. We must find a terminology which enables us to give expression to the dynamic element in the ecumenical situation. There is still a great deal of hard theological work to be done in order to clarify our position. We are in danger of using certain formulas without thinking through the precise significance and limitation of these formulas."[37]

Certainly, for Visser't Hooft, the biblical perspective is more helpful than theological formulas. It relates in the work of God renewal and unity, the gathering of a people wholly consecrated to Him. That divine work of gathering must continue in the life of the Church, for the human forces which endanger its wholeness are still at work. The oneness of the renewed Church must be a sign to the world. It must become visible in the life of the Church, almost the tangible characteristic of the <u>Koinonia</u>. True unity cannot be a static unity; it must be the manifestation of the activity of Christ, the Great Shepherd of the Church. Visser't Hooft reaffirms this idea that renewal and gathering are possible only in the power of the Word, as follows: "Again to be gathered by the Lord is to be renewed, to receive new life, and so to be enabled to render the witness which the world needs. In other words the statements about unity we seek to make in the World Council are simply implications of that biblical <u>Kerygma</u> which is our common basis and criterion." And again: ... we believe in unity sought in obedience to the revealed Will of God for His Church and with deep concern for both the purity and the missionary outreach of the Church. We do not stand for some vague unity of our own invention. We stand for the unity given by the Chief Shepherd who knows only one flock."[38]

The concept of unity cannot be vague, althought it remains an object of faith. Speaking of the relation of the local church to the <u>Una Sancta</u>, Visser't Hooft reconciles what seems paradoxical; the Church believes in a given unity not yet fully manifested in history, but clearly intended an revealed by Christ. Unity must be visible as the Church itself is visible. We should remain alert to the danger of a utopian ecumenicity.

Visser't Hooft suggests that utopianism can take many forms. Many Christians have a wrong, narrow, and secularized conception of the Church. Their vision of the Church has no supernatural dimension; it is almost deprived of all theological content. It corresponds to a utilitarian concept of Christianity. The Church is the Church of man, a servant of men's dreams. It is not the real Church, but an association of like-minded people capable of producing some kind of pragmatic ecumenical activism. In that context, church union can be understood only in terms of a federation of churches. Such ecumenicity is imaginary in so far as it does not exemplify the unity given by Christ. It is found at the 'grassroot' level. "The real sense of the Church has been lost in all our churches, even in those which have officially a high conception of the Church. We are confronted everywhere by that basic heresy of possessiveness, of men thinking that they can claim ownership of the things that belong to God. There has been in our day and age a rediscovery of the Church of God, but it is still largely confined to theological circles. At the level of the parish we are as it were in the pre-church epoch, in the era of individualism in which the Church is judged by its success in meeting what men consider their needs, in which few feel in their hearts and know in their minds that the Church is the Church of God, God's own People."[39]

In the group of those who know the Church as God's own People many are the victims of another form of utopian ecumenicity. Very often the ecumenically alert Christian believes that he has at least seen the true Church. Theologically he is more sensitive to the implications of the teaching of the New Testament which he cannot reconcile with the reality of church life as it exists. The danger for him is to look at a Church in the clouds. Unity, then, is to be reached in its purity beyond the historical churches. Reality is sacrificed to an ideal. Visser't Hooft suggests that some utopian ecumenists can fall into "ecclesiastical docetism: "The Una Sancta can become and is becoming an alibi for large numbers of Christians. They refuse to take the Church around the corner or the historically given churches seriously, because these do not correspond to the ideal Church which they have discovered in and through the ecumenical movement. There is real danger that the number of such uprooted Christians will grow. There is the danger that we get an ecclesiastical docetism which accepts the idea of the Church, but refuse to live with and in the reality of the Church. It is a disquieting sign of the times that while interest in the ecumenical movement grows all the time, we hear from many countries that Church attendance decreases."[40]

The eschatological dimension of the Kingdom does not mean that the Church is invisible or otherwordly or exclusively belonging to the future. We have seen how in the biblical perspective the new age has entered into the old. The Church is a visible and tangible reality; so must be its unity. To believe in the Church is not to believe in a utopia. Because the true Church is not an invention of man but a work of God we must believe that it exists here and now.[41] Of course, what we see is not the One, Holy Church; it is divided, and different churches have different answers to the problem of their relation to the Una Sancta. But the unity of that Church is not a dream but a reality. Naturally, this is an affirmation of faith: "We know that the one God can only have one people and that Christ cannot be divided. We believe therefore that there is, in spite of what we see, one single Church of God. The unity of the Church is more real than its divisions because it is one in the mind and will of God."[42]

We have established the need for Church renewal on facts: first, that the Church is composed of sinners; second, that the Church has been guilty of collective sins. The Church stands in constant need of renewal. For the same reason says Visser't Hooft, the Church needs to be constantly gathered by its Shepherd. The Church like the individual Christian is at the same time justified and sinner; consequently it is both renewed and corrupted, one and divided. At all times, however, it is in the hands of God; the Holy Spirit is constantly at work in the life of the Church.

This attitude of faith has many practical implications. Visser't Hooft stresses what could be called a common-sense approach to the life of the Church. The Church on earth will always remain human and subject to the flunctuations of human nature: "We cannot and must not expect to find in this world a church which in its empirical existence manifests in complete purity the splendour of the Bride of Christ 'without spot or wrinkle.' It means that we must not turn away from the Church simply because it does not correspond to the vision of the Una Sancta which we have received from the New Testament."[43]

It is true that no Christians today can join a fully renewed and fully united Church of Christ on earth. No Church, in its particularism, is the true society of the reconciled; for no Church embraces the whole People of God.[44] It remains imperative, however, that all Christians in their denominations should face the responsibility of working for the visible manifestation of the Una Sancta: "... the one and only way to work for a full manifestation of the unity of the Church is to work for it within the life of our churches, and when we are called to oppose, our opposition will be a loyal opposition."[45]

Visser't Hooft is very impatient with those ready to try easy or immediate solutions to the problem of disunity. He refuses to follow those who consider "that it must be possible to find some short cut to the visible manifestation of the Una Sancta."[46] Only a complete misunderstanding of the Church, regarded as an invisible reality, would allow us to say that our divisions have no significance. We are not one in Jesus Christ as long as we refuse to break out of the limits of denominationalism. Visser't Hooft rejects as another form of utopian ecumenicity the idea that all Christian Churches together represent the Una Sancta. Differences between Churches cannot be regarded as mere varieties. They do not enrich the common life of the Church of Christ, as some would claim. For Visser't Hooft such a position on unity is not defendable in the light of Scriptures. "We cannot say that because we are not ignorant of what the New Testament means by unity, and it is clear that our differences in faith and our separateness in order deny the unity which the Church of Christ is meant to have."[47]

The historical Churches, however, are part of the 'given.' They represent the 'Locus' of God's action. It is only through a process of transformation and renewal that the gift of unity will become a living reality. Visser't Hooft is clear on that point.

To seek for unity outside the Church is to end in a blind-alley.

The problem, however, is that after sixty years of ecumenism thehistorical churches are not ready for unity. They are unwilling to take a step into the unknown. They do not want to lose something essential, namely the joy of understanding themselves as the Church of Christ. They have a strong fear of a monolithic Church, of a Super-Church which would suppress all freedom. Surely the churches realize that there is a gap between the truth they teach and the reality of their life, between the reconciliation they proclaim and the separateness they condone. They know that it is the raison d'être of the Church to demonstrate the full unity which belongs to the Body of Christ. But they attach too much importance, according to Visser't Hooft, to irrelevant factors that keep them apart. One can feel a certain impatience in reading the following lines: "I call irrelevant factors all those that are not rooted in convictions concerning God's revelation in Christ. In other words all considerations that have to do with our social, national, racial, cultural, organizational preferences and prejudices. For none of these can be of any weight when we are clearly told that it belongs to the nature of the Church to be one."[48]

The very life of the koinonia rests upon a willingness to share the gifts of grace. This is true also of the relations between churches in their quest for unity. We look to the Church as a body; and the 'Body' to be one must grow into Christ and each part must be working properly. True unity must be in accord with Jesus Christ. "If our Lord counts unity a necessity, how absolute must that necessity be. Upon it depends our ability to know Jesus Christ in his full splendour, to do his work, to evangelize the nations."[49]

Unity and Liberty

We come now to the existential problem of the relation of unity to liberty. Visser't Hooft has repeated time and again that the ecumenical movement does not want to be a Super-Church; and whoever has read him and the declarations of the World Council of Churches has no doubt about the sincerity of modern ecumenicity. Many Christians and Churches, however, still deeply distrust all movements for Christian unity. The tragic experience of history have left a deep mark upon the Christian conscience of the world. The apocalyptic vision of Babylon (Rev.17) is still frightening many quarters of the Church. The spector of an ecclesiastical institution which has secular power at his disposal is still present before the eyes of many. Visser't Hooft is perfectly aware that some of the most crucial crisis of Western history were struggles for liberation from the evils of a Super-Church. He writes: "The conflict between the Emperors and the Popes, the Reformation in its political aspects, the Thirty Years War, the reaction against Louis XIV and the Glorious Revolution, the resistance against the Holy Alliance are all in one way or another inspired by the conviction that the monopolistic all-powerful Church represents a tremendous danger. And the heroes who have fought these great battles such as Emperor Frederick II, King Gustavus Adolphus or King William I are known to us as champions of liberty."[50]

In the World Council of Churches many churches were at one time the victims of a super-church mentality; and some national churches assumed the role of a super-church and persecuted minority-churches. Today, however, all member-churches oppose the re-emergence of a centralized ecclesiastical world body. All would recognize the great danger of the Super-Church in the definition suggested by Visser't Hooft. "The Super-Church is a centralized ecclesiastical institution of world-wide character which seeks to impose unity and uniformity by means of outward pressure and political influence and thus denies the New Testament conception of the Church of Christ."[51]

The Ecumenical Movement does not dream of the re-establishment of a Corpus Christianum demanding a monopolistic position.[52] It stands in favour of religious liberty and denounces the danger of institutionalism. It carefully avoids all identification of the Church, as the People of God, with an ecclesiastical body; and it warns the Churches that with their empirical life being subjected to the laws of sociology, it is easy for them to become bureaucratically oriented and preoccupied. "The danger of the Super-Church lies in its introversion, its preoccupation with the maintenance of its traditional forms of life, its transformation of means into ends, its unwillingness to let itself be fundamentally renewed."

Furthermore, the Ecumenical Movement refuses to look on unity as an aim in itself. Unity must be seen in relation to the truth that the Gospel cannot be imposed on man or society by outward pressure and that unity can be Christian only in the context of freedom.[54]

Critics of the World Council of Churches, however, do not recognize the concern for freedom in the life of the movement. Some fundamentalist groups regard the Council as a new Babylon, as association of apostate churches. Visser't Hooft acknowledges the fact with some disappointment. "Their view is that there will be an increasingly definite realization of the apocalyptic vision and that this will take the form of a universal ecclesiastical organization including Rome or dominated by Rome and manifesting the great apostasy. Since it is also believed that the World Council is on the way to create such a centralized, all-embracing ecclesiastical body the conclusion seems to be evident: the W.C.C. is a modern incarnation of the apocalyptic Babylon."[55]

Therefore, it is important to insist that the concern for unity is not tied to any secular concern. That the Church of

Christ is one is a biblical affirmation. Perhaps for the first time in history churches are coming together because they believe in Unity as a sign of Christ's presence in their midst and of the renewal of their life. Since Amsterdam the Council has been quite clear. Many of its activities have to do with Church renewal; none is involved in negotiating union between Churches. The aim of the Council is to bring churches into contact with each other that they may grow together in Christ and receive from Him the gift of Unity.[56] The Ecumenical Movement fosters unity by means of spiritual renewal. Of course the World Council of Churches "exerts a real influence and develops a certain ethos;"[57] but the danger of a Super-Church will be successfully overcome as long as we realize that "every advance toward unity must be accompanied by a corresponding advance in the purification of the churches from all conscious or subconscious desire for power. The spiritual implication of true unity is that a united Church must be able to withstand the temptation which any increase in influence or power may bring with it."[58]

Unity and Pluralism

Desire for power, however, is very difficult to eradicate; and in the situation of a united Christianity it could represent-- at least in the eyes of many--a danger to the world. The world has always been pluralistic.[59] The Western world, however, has not always been conscious of that fact, especially when it constituted a monolithic Christendom. After the Reformation pluralism was noted as a phenomenon within a common tradition. The development of modern pluralism in the West is due to many factors. One of the most important is the continuing process of secularization. In the first chapter we said how the Church had lost its monopolistic position in society. New social and cultural forces act independently from all religious authority to create new values and new standards. This does not mean *de facto* the end of religion. Visser't Hooft argues that "secularization does not necessarily lead to secularism. It leads most often to pluralism."[60] It means the emergence of non-religious centers of influence in the world, which give a new impetus to pluralism. To this day they have failed, however, to eliminate religion, although they are used against it. Visser't Hooft remarks that religion has shown a surprising survival instinct. "The late 19th century prophecies that the Roman Catholic Church was a dying Church; the Marxist prophecies concerning the inevitable disappearance of religion in communist societies; the national socialist hopes that the Churches could be eliminated, have all proved completely false. In fact the secularization process has often meant that the Church found new freedom and new vigour. In other words secularization means the emergence of a world situation in which there is a new polarization of fundamental convictions and a baffling variety of choices."[61]

In the light of that new order, the Christian Churches have subscribed to the principle of religious liberty and freedom of conscience. Even the Roman Catholic Church supports now this most fundamental human right.[62] Pluralism can be in fact, a "blessing in disguise" a cure to many spiritual ills. We must recognize its good as well as its potential danger: "it is quite clear, says Visser't Hooft, that pluralism is not going to make our lives any easier. But I believe that we should not waste our time regretting the simpler situation of the past. I believe especially that Christians should not dream of returning to times when their faith was the one, officially and generally accepted, standard of the common life. For pluralism provides a very real opportunity for a deep revision of Christian attitudes which has been long overdue. Pluralism is the cure which Christianity needs badly."[63]

Today the non-religious as well as the religious advocate their own conception of life and develop their own ethos. The theological and the philosophical understandings of the human condition have equal rights, if not *de facto* equal opportunity. Both contribute to a wider pluralism. Very often national cultures define their identity by stressing their ancient religious traditions this explains the renaissance of Hinduism and Buddhism, for instance. It has traditionally been the case of Judaism.

How long such a renaissance will last; it is difficult to say. In a nationalistic historical context it may, in fact, lead to other forms of secularism.

The question of interest for us is Visser't Hooft's views on the relation of unification and pluralism. Can the latter be a product of the former? Yes and no. Ideologies are no longer restricted by geographical boundaries. They all take a universal dimension.[64] By doing so they bring men into closer inter-relationships; they create a certain pattern of world-unification. However, it is not necessarily so; for man has been influenced by pluralism and understands himself in the same pattern of thought. As an example, Visser't Hooft points to the case of Roman-Catholicism in the Latin countries.[65] In Italy, it is possible for a Catholic to go to Mass on Sunday, and yet to be a supporter of the Communist Party. No religion, no Church, no party can claim any more to represent the convictions of a whole people. In a sense, no one can represent all the aspirations of a man. The tension between unification and pluralism is a phenomenon in the life of the modern world. It exists, says Visser't Hooft. Perhaps, the Churches are the victim of that tension; and yet they contributed to its rise in trying to prevent it. The old monolithic societies, the <u>Corpora Christiana</u>, in which Church, state and community were inseparable and overlapping were, in fact, maintaining the church in a tight embrace in which it could not breathe and act freely. Thus the movements of renewal in the church--whether of more pietistic or of more ecclesiocentric origin--all tended to give to the church again its own distinct function and place. Free churches arose and fought for equal rights with the established churches. But once this right was granted the way to the wider pluralism had been opened."[66]

The Churches still find it difficult to accept that pluralism which points to their declining influence in the world. The Christian society is no longer a reality; in that sense one can speak of a post-Christian era. Visser't Hooft suggests that the Churches should recognize this fact without renouncing their claim that the Gospel is universal and the Kingship of Christ cosmic in its scope. The World Council of Churches distinguishes now, quite clearly, between the universal Lordship of Christ--the core of the Gospel--and Catholic universalism--a dream of the past.[67]

Here, once again, Visser't Hooft expresses his conviction that the Church should not yield to the temptation of returning to the concept of Christendom. Such a dream of restoration come true would be in fact, a step backward perhaps to a worse form of secularization. "The trouble with the old situation was that Christianity was taken to be self-evident. Everybody was of course a Christian. Those who could not bring themselves to accept the Christian faith seemed to be perverted. But in such a situation faith is no longer faith. It is no longer a commitment to a living truth, to a discovered reality: it is a going along, an acceptance of what society has decided for me. The break-down of Christianity as a general social convention is the opportunity to give to faith again its original meaning: the meaning of risk and choice and personal answer."[68]

The dream of restoration would prevent the Church from facing perhaps its greatest challenge in history. The disintegration of a certain type of Christian society does not necessarily mean that man subscribes to the idea that he can live without religion; and other religions are not, per se, the enemies of Christianity. Visser't Hooft says that: "We need a new Christian civilization and it is perfectly possible to pass from a traditional type of Christian society to a renewed Christian society without passing through the stage of dechristianization."[69]

Under the new conditions of intellectual and political freedom, the Church cannot be reinstated as the only integrating force in society. The Church could not ask the state to act as defensor fidei without forsaking its own freedom. Visser't Hooft said that to be renewed the Church had to face its strangeness and accept that it be bound only to its Lord. "Now pluralism means that no Church, no philosophy can run the show. The Church is thrown back on its true task. It can only live as a servant-Church. That does not mean a withdrawal from society, but it means a different form of presence in society. As it is less and less mixed up with the status quo, it receives greater freedom to experiment. As it does not have to defend its social and political position it receives a new flexibility. As its influence on society is no longer exercised in the form of a generally accepted social control, it must necessarily concentrate on the forming of individual Christians who in their daily work can bring Christion convictions into the life of society."[70]

This does not mean introversion and withdrawal. The Church would be wrong to conclude that a pluralistic world is demonic. It must continue, however, to proclaim that God's intervention in history through Jesus Christ represents a unique redemptive force. The Church cannot deny its prophetic ministry in and to the world. It must continue to speak, successfully or not, a liberating word to man. It must express a judgment on social and political issues and defend the rights of all men. The mission of the Church remains valid, even when all doors are closed. "We know that the prophet cannot be an opportunist in the ordinary sense of that word, because he is made aware of an opportunity created by God who over-rules the calculations of men. Here again success or failure are not decisive categories. Nor need a Church be influential or powerful to speak the liberating word to the people."[71]

Furthermore, in a pluralistic world, the Church should not abandon the notion of unique truth. That pluralism be a fact should not lead man to accept pluralism as a philosophy of life, "a cure for all ills."[72] Truth has its own objectivity and validity independently of its recognition by men. Religious liberty means that man must live responsibly and choose. Christ is still asking the world: "Whom do you think I am?" (Mt. 16:15) Ultimately, the answer must be that of rejection or discipleship. The great danger of pluralism is to become a form of escapism; it is to "breed a race of spiritually spineless human beings who would live in the sort of night in which all cats are grey."[73]

Visser't Hooft rejects relativism. He understands Vatican II, which opened its decree on religious freedom with a confession of faith: "that God himself has made known to mankind the way in which men are to serve Him, and thus be saved in Christ and come to blessedness. We believe that this one true religion subsists in the catholic and apostolic Church, to which the Lord Jesus committed the duty of spreading its abroad among all men."[74]

Visser't Hooft remarks that man cannot live deprived of all absolute. When the religious absolute weakens or dies out, other absolutes may develop in different areas. A political ideology, for instance, may grow into an absolute. Man is looking for an all-encompassing truth, giving an answer to the basic questions of the meaning of life.

Some will object, however, that the quest for an absolute in a pluralistic world may lead to ideological conflicts. Rather, they argue that the new pattern of world-unification would demand a common ethos, based on an agreement about the ultimate issues of truth. None of the historic religions and common philosophies can be accepted as normative. The world-community, therefore, can reconcile unification and pluralism only in the context of syncretism. Even if such a thesis sounds naive, it cannot be dismissed too promptly. Christianity is responsible to some extent for its rise. Visser't Hooft comments: "The fact that many of the attempts to elaborate a universal synthesis are superficial and naive does not necessarily mean that the concept of world-religion is to be rejected. And we Christians have, advocating Christianity, so often used the argument that a world faith is absolutely indispensable for the life of humanity, that we have no right to laugh about people who use similar arguments and who come, in the light of the present situation, to the conclusion that that world religion must be a mixture between Christianity and other religions."[75]

Christianity, however, being essentially a prophetic religion, must defend the integrity of its nature and mission. Religion cannot be a political means; it cannot be used to unify the world. Such religion would be only a religion of man; a religion in which humanity would adore itself.[76] A religion of man in the hands of men would easily become intolerant, an instrument to curtail individual liberties. Man can add a new dimension to his religious experience by learning to live in a pluralistic environment. Between two evils--a relativist pluralism and the imposition of a world ideology--the former is the lesser one. Reflecting upon history, Visser't Hooft has this to say: "We must not forget that the great temptation of an all-powerful religion is to suppress religious minorities and that numerous inter-religious conflicts have been caused precisely by the attempt to make one religion a world religion without competitors. The plurality of religions and ideologies brings with it infinite possibilities of misunderstanding and conflicts, but attempts to force the situation by the imposition of one religion or ideology make the situation worse."[77]

The tension, however, remains; for it is the mission of the Church to lead the whole world to Christ. But pluralism is not a danger for the true calling of the Church. On the contrary, suggests Visser't Hooft. In a situation of minority, the Church can be truly renewed and united in its obedience to the Lord. In past history the concept of Christendom has been a curse rather than a blessing. Privileges have bound the Church to the world. Political ambitions have corrupted it. The new motto 'let the Church be the Church' is a plea for freedom from all the entangling alliances of the so-called 'Christian society' with the secular society. The Church becomes the Church when it is supported only by God. Once again, renewal is the answer to our problem.

Visser't Hooft suggests that pluralism may indirectly help the Church to be renewed and united under its Lord. He remarks that: "Pluralism rightly understood creates for the church a situation in which it is less in danger of falsifying its own nature and in which it is better able to manifest its true calling. Pluralism provides the Church with a God-given opportunity to live according to its own inherent spiritual law."[78]

An important aspect of that "inherent spiritual law" of the Church is freedom for the individual to express his own convictions in the Christian community. And the same community should respect the freedom of those outside the Church. Opposition to the Church, from inside and outside, may lead to greater renewal and to the "clarification of the true nature of the Christian faith."[79] All special privileges should be renounced unless they be shared by all churches and groups. In fact they should be avoided as a temptation to facility and complacency. Special recognition of one church is also dangerous; for it threatens or limits the freedom of minority groups and makes of religious freedom a mockery. "The sooner we arrive at true equality of opportunity for all spiritual and philosophical families, the better for the health of our mutual relationship.[80] In so far as renewal changes or affects a human institution, it brings with it periods of transition, questioning and even sectarian fanaticism. Only strong convictions can renew the Church; only an honest dialogue will bring the Church closer to unity. Silence, compromise, or weakness "... are consciously or unconsciously promoting a secularistic type of uniformity which discriminates against all positive beliefs and is thus on the way to create a spineless indifferentism."[81]

In a pluralistic world, Christians and Churches are engaged in a spiritual battle for truth. In that encounter, they should remain open-minded, but not at the price of what Visser't Hooft calls "le choc des opinions."[82] It is possible for churches, today more than ever, to disagree on essential issues and continue to live and work together. This is now true of the relationship between Christian Churches; and it is already true of the relationship between religions.[83] Indeed a world-community remains a dream. It is, however, a positive dream in so far as it is calling men back to deep concern for unity. Visser't Hooft suggests that "a pluralistic world-society is too tough for a divided church."[84] This, of course, cannot be a sufficient cause for unity; but it can help the churches to look on pluralism as a blessing in disguise. "The pluralistic world throws us all back on the primary source of our faith and forces us to take a new look at the world around us. Thus pluralism can provide a real opportunity for a new united witness of the whole Church of Christ in and to the world."[85]

The Oecumenical Society[86]

It is possible to speak of unity? Churches have already agreed that unity cannot be made by men; it can only be received from God by a renewed Church. Unity is a reality in which we believe. Visser't Hooft, writing on the eve of the Oxford Conference in 1937, presented the Church Universal as the "critical principle" in the life of all Churches engaged in the quest for unity. It throws light on the failure of the churches to be the Church of Christ, on God's judgment and promise. "...the Church Universal remains a reality in which we believe. As such it is the great critical principle in the life of all Churches. The very great value of the oecumenical movement consists in the fact that it reminds us by its very existence of the challenge of the criticism. In its light we see more clearly how much our Churches have become entangled with the world of nations and races and classes, and how little they have lived up to their faith in the Church Universal. In its light also we discover what elements in our divisions are no more than very relative cultural or other human idiosyncrasies which have no right to hold the Churches apart. In its light we become troubled in our consciences about the self-satisfaction and complacency of our Churches, and learn to pray that God may give us the unity which we ourselves are unable to realize."[87]

Unfortunately our deep disagreement as to the nature and function of the Church obscures our agreement as to the reality of the Church of Christ. Writing also at the same period, Karl Barth suggested that the "where, who and what is the Church?"[88] remained the most serious question faced by the ecumenical movement. The movement itself has no ecclesiology of its own. Member-churches should neither impose their particular standpoint upon the Council nor renounce it. In their desire to act corporately, the Churches should resist the temptation of finding agreement on Christian witness irrespective of doctrine and ecclesiology. Any standpoint which would transcend all existing ecclesiologies would prove to be an over-simplification of the real problem. More than twenty years after the Oxford Conference the data of the problem have not changed. The ecumenical movement is facing the same issue; and what Visser't Hooft wrote then, is still relevant: "The difficult reality is that there is no 'oecumenical' conception of the Church which can be accepted by all (or even by a large majority) of the Churches. The very essence of the oecumenical problem is precisely that the Churches are not at one on this basic matter, and that no Church can claim to represent in itself the solution of the oecumenical problem. It is a condition *sine qua non* of any oecumenical work that each Church, and the oecumenical movement as a whole, should realize this fact, and not try to cover it up by ambiguous language which means differentthings to different people. It is only by a frank facing of real differences that advance can be made in the realm of Christian co-operation and unity."[89]

The question of unity cannot be isolated from the question of truth. The ecumenical movement is aware of the fact that the various conceptions of the Church we have mentioned earlier are not merely complementing each other, but also are contradictory. Even the 'branch' theory proves unsatisfactory. It denies the validity of the 'catholic' ecclesiology of those churches which claim each to be 'the true church'; and if it were adopted by the Council it would close the door to them. Furthermore, it subscribes, at least implicitly, to "a conception of tolerance which owes its origins, not to the Bible, but to modern humanitarianism."[90] The quest for unity at the expense of truth can be a sinful fascination of universalism. Karl Barth reminded the Churches in 1937 that unity in itself will never suffice; indeed it is against God's will unless it becomes a common quest of the Churches for Jesus Christ: "The quest for the unity of the Church must not be a quest for Church-unity in itself; for as such it is idle and empty. On the road to such a 'Church-unity in itself' we shall find that both the powers of sin and the powers of grace are against us, and against us irresistibly."[91]

Christ is the oneness of the Church; in Christ there is a multiplicity of gifts, persons, and communities, but not a multiplicity of churches. It is in that oneness in Christ that the Church finds life, calling and relevance. The only acceptable multiplicity is that which is rooted in unity. Any other form of multiplicity is a form of incompleteness. Faith in Jesus Christ brings with it the implication that we belong no longer to ourselves but to Him and share in His oneness. In other words, faith in Christ implies our responsibility of working together towards the uniting of His Church. The attitude of the Churches cannot be defined in terms of tolerance, respect and co-operation, but in terms of the readiness to hear and to understand each other. Ultimately the union of the Churches will mean "a union of the confessions into one unanimous Confession."[92] Such unity, however, cannot be reached at the price of confessional weakness. We live in a situation of separatedness. It is in our own particular Church that we listen to Christ, not in another Church or in a situation of theological neutrality. We all raise the problems of Church, doctrine, order, and Christian life in the existential context of our divisions. At the very beginning of our journey toward union we must endorse the confession of our own Church. It expresses our relation to Christ and his Church. Indeed, it is a matter of loyalty. Visser't Hooft has always been quite clear on that subject. Just before the Oxford Conference, he wrote: "It is precisely because we have to do with nothing less than the Church which is the Body of Christ that we dare not think in terms of opportunism or compromises. The reasons why we should bury our divisions, and present a truly united front to the world, are indeed pressing and weighty. No one who has

CHAPTER V

RENEWAL AND WHOLENESS

The Christian and the Church

Renewal and unity are, for Visser't Hooft, steps forward for the manifestation of the wholeness of the Church; and in the corporate reality of the Church the wholeness of the Christian conditions that of the community. Hence the three subdivisions of this last chapter: first, the relationship of renewal and unity to wholeness, second, the wholeness of the Christian, third the wholeness of the Church.

The Relationship of Renewal and Unity to Wholeness

The problem of renewal and church unity is essentially related to the concept of wholeness. The Church is "an undivided whole which is the Body of Christ."[1] To belong to Christ is to be part of his body. Visser't Hooft has told us repeatedly that it is impossible to think of "a direct relationship with Christ without participation in the whole Church of Christ."[2] And this is true of the relationship of the particular congregation to the Church catholic. We receive from the New Testament a vision of wholeness; and we believe that it is God's purpose to restore it through renewal and reunion. Without such a dream or vision the World Council of Churches would have no raison d'être left. The Christian churches are coming together is some measure of oneness because of the conviction that the one Church of Christ is a living reality: "Nothing that has happened in the history of the Church has changed or can change the basic fact that there is one single Church of Christ and that, whether we can see it or not, its life is the life of a coherent whole, the parts of which are inseparably related to each other and mutually interdependent."[3]

Isolated from the Church of Christ a church can only wither; and the whole body itself suffers from the present state of things. In the Church of Christ divisiveness means sickness, while unity is a sign of wholeness. The very existence of the World Council of Churches is a witness to the twofold truth: "that our Churches do not really live up to their great mission as convincing witness to the existence of the one Body of Christ and that God, in spite of our division, sees His Church as a whole and does not cease to work for the manifestation of its wholeness."[4]

In their quest for renewal the Churches should strive to overcome their self-centeredness. To that end they must live by the grace of God. Commenting on the twelfth chapter of the first letter of the Corinthians, Visser't Hooft translate _charisma_ by "gift of grace." Charisma [is] a God-given function or task together with the power to fulfill that task. [...] It is to be used in and for the whole Church of Christ."

In the fellowship of the Church the gifts of grace imparted by the Spirit to individuals must be shared by all for the strengthening of the whole Body. We see immediately how the renewal of Christians is a _conditio sine qua non_ of the wholeness of the Church; "for the New Testament conceives of Churches as corporate personalities."[6] Conversely the wholeness of the Christian is possible only in the fellowship of a renewed Church. In 1937 Visser't Hooft wrote <u>None Other Gods</u>[7] which deals precisely with that problem of individual renewal. One may wonder why it comes so late in our study. It is a deliberate choice based, we hope, on a correct interpretation of Visser't Hooft. The corporate character of Christianity places the body above its members and emphasizes the all-comprehensive dimension of a total relationship. The <u>charismata</u> of Christian life are received by believers within the fellowship. They are part of the 'given' to the whole Church.

The Wholeness of the Christian

In our religious perspective, wholeness is a matter of choice for or against God whom we meet in Jesus Christ. It is a matter of personal decision and commitment. Choosing is an essential manifestation of life. Visser't Hooft likes to paraphrase Pascal's concern to make of faith an act of the will: "... to be alive is to choose, and the refusal to choose is really the refusal to accept the peculiar responsibility of conscious living."[8]

We bear the moral burden of choice.[9] The philosophical presuppositions of it cannot be established on evidence. We accept no external standard of authority in our quest for truth; this is obvious in the question of faith which deals with an ultimate choice.[10]   Faith is the basis of all other choices; it is based on nothing other than itself. Visser't Hooft stresses that any belief in God acceptable to reason would not really be faith in God, but rather faith in reason. He comments: "The ultimate choice, whatever it may be, is then neither rational nor scientific nor sentimental. It precedes and transcends these other human realms. It is truly an act of faith, in that it carries within it an element of pure adventure, and excludes the possibility of demonstrable proof or of secure guarantees against error."[11]

Like Pascal in L'Argument du Pari, Visser't Hooft accepts the risk of faith: the risk must be taken "not in the abstract domain of cold ideas, but in the concrete realm of throbbing life."[12]   The choice of faith must be faced at the level of 'being'; it is the choice of Jesus Christ. We choose a person in whom we meet God. And God is above religion--actually Visser't Hooft suggests that we must decide between God and religion. He claims that religion is only a phenomenon belonging to life. It is distinguished from other phenomena in that it is related to something considered as ultimate.[13]   It is a form; and the typical error is to identify the form with the content. Indeed religion may become a substitute for a higher reality. "As God seems to recede into His high heaven, men grope for something more tangible. And religion which resembles at least in form, if not in content, the relationship to God, is the most likely choice as a new foundation of life."[14]

Religion may also come to be regarded as an inclusive phenomenon of all the historic religions; unity is then misunderstood to represent a lower common denominator of an "incoherent mass of religious phenomena."[15] Visser't Hooft rejects the concept of 'religion' in the singular. Historical religions could be reduced to a synthesis only at the price of their identity, uniqueness, and wholeness. Such a synthesis could not serve any useful purpose; for it could not be considered to be an ultimate or an absolute: "...The bringing together of absolutes is only possible by transforming them into relatives. In other words, a Religion in which all men agree can be brought into being only by the eradication of all historic or positive religions."[16]

The Christian concerned to maintain his identity should be alert to a twofold fact. First, he lives in a world where Christianity is surrounded and challenged by other religions; secondly, he is appealed to by many other non-religious conceptions of life, which openly profess to be alternatives to the Christian faith. Can a Christian retain his 'wholeness' and at the same time welcome all thoughts susceptible to being included in traditional and authentic Christianity? Or should he, as some do, dismiss all religious thoughts as pure illusions. The Christian is tempted in many ways. Although there is no general consensus of opinion, many people of the educated classes of the old Christian

Western World subscribe to a pure form of relativism. They claim that the ways of truth are many; no particular doctrine or system, therefore, should be erected in an absolute. All conceptions of life have some element of truth in them. They are all helpful in directing man toward his ultimate end. Their best ideological values, therefore, should be combined into "one imposing symphony of truth."[17] But, according to Visser't Hooft, as soon as we become open to the greatest possible variety of truths we reject the inherent value of Christianity and make of it a relativist religion. The Gospel loses its wholeness; it becomes diluted in a vague subjective religiosity. We assume then that: "man can find salvation in various faiths and through different rites, provided he directs his soul toward the principle of divinity, loves his fellowman, and translates his love into deeds of justice and charity."[18]

Consequently, the mission of the Church is denied; for if there is no essential distinction between the revealed truth in Christianity and the truth of other religious traditions, the missionary enterprise becomes superfluous. The only possible message of the Church would be: "Let everyone find his salvation in his own way."[19] This, of course, would be the end of Christianity; as soon as the content of faith becomes secondary, religion itself is being affected by the reduction process. Basically it becomes either a system of ethics or an emotional attitude: "The inclusive attitude presupposes a conception of Christianity and of religion generally which looks upon the contents of faith as secondary. For it the distinctive thing about religion is either an ethical or an emotional attitude. Religion is either that function of human life which acts as the great moral dynamic to 'make the world a better place to live in,' or that peculiar sphere of life where man finds its deepest emotional satisfaction. On both bases a thoroughly tolerant non-aggressive and purely cooperative attitude to other views of life may be worked out. For if I believe that the ultimate goal of religion is to work for a better world, why should I not join efforts with those of other religions who are interested in the same goal and why should I not welcome their teachings on the same subject as long as they seem to point in the same direction? And again, if I believe that religion's task is to give man emotional satisfaction, why should I not accept the greatest variety of contributions of all religions to the great cause of giving inward peace to mankind?"[20]

Visser't Hooft rejects such presuppositions. They are in contradiction with the very foundation of Christianity, namely that Christ is the truth (Jn. 14:6) and the sole ground of salvation (Acts 4:12). God has revealed Himself to man in Jesus Christ (Heb. 1:2). Christianity is not primarily concerned with an ethical dynamic for a better world, but with a person. Christianity is the religion of Christ. The Christian hears a call to discipleship; he is confronted with a personal relationship. Jesus says

"Follow me." (Mt. 4:19) "He does not merely ask us to accept his moral principles and to imitate his life; he calls us to enter into the Kingdom of God, in which God is no longer vaguely believed in as a mysterious power of good, but is believed in as a Father whose will we can know and whose love we can accept."[21]

The encounter with Jesus Christ is the crucial event of the life of the believer, the center of his religious experience and the sure orientation of his hope. It is really what matters to man in Christianity. Nothing is true in religion unless it can stand the test of God's self-revelation to man in Christ. This position remains very subjective to those who are looking at Christianity from the outside. This position is relative and fallible. Seen from inside, however, a decision for Christ means that truth ultimately comes to us in the form of a person. Visser't Hooft writes: "The decisive question with which humanity is faced is not whether God exists but whether He is personal. It is a sign of the weakness of present-day Christianity that this is so little recognized. [...] 'Do we believe in a personal God?' The question is by no means a theoretical one. I cannot believe in a personal God unless He exists for me as a real person, that is as a 'thou'. I cannot decide the question by speculation because even if all evidence of the world forced me to think of God as personal, while I have not actually met Him as a personal Will in my life, the question remains unanswered. To believe in a personal God means that we have come face to face with one, who speaks and acts in our lives."[22]

In an atmosphere of relativity, this is difficult to understand. Religion has been depersonalized; we think in terms of law and ideas. Visser't Hooft remarks that many, who reject the absolute of faith, maintain that "Religion is a matter of accepting such human and super-human realities as can be scientifically proved to exist and to be truly useful to mankind."[23]

But Christianity is centered around the event of the incarnation; the God-Man. Visser't Hooft recognizes that "It is hard for relativistic moderns to believe that God should have spoken in time and space, and that there is one point in history which is not merely an event in the endless chain of events but the very center of history."[24]

The choice for Jesus Christ remains, however, the cornerstone of Christianity. In Christ we transcend Religion, we come to know God himself. "Christianity is God-centeredness, and not just interest in religion."[25] The Gospel rejects in religion what is purely a human product. Visser't Hooft can assume, therefore, that God is opposed to the Christian religion whenever that religion begins to be self-centered; whenever Christianity as a religon becomes more important than Christianity as a relationship with God. The Christian must make a definite choice between God and religion. "For in the first case we expect everything from the insights and discoveries of man himself. In the first case we live by revelation, that is by God communicating his truth to us; in the second case we live by producing ourselves the truth which will guide us."[26]

The real question remains, however, as to the inclusive character of Christianity. What may the Christian include in his religious experience without becoming disobedient to his Lord? The wholeness of what has been given to men through Christ must be preserved. Visser't Hooft says: "We must part company with those who look upon their faith as a thing of their own making and who are accordingly willing to accept or reject, to include and to exclude other religious values according to their own free choice and liking. We must dare to confess that the greatest thing about our faith is that which has been given to us and we must be ready to be obedient to Him Who gave it. His truth is put in our hands. We may not be worthy of it, we may only perceive it at times, we may deny it by our lives or spoil it by the admixture of our impurity and weakness--but it remains at the bottom His truth."[27]

The divine truth, received in faith, does not need defense. Of course, the Christian must look critically upon his own thoughts and actions. He must remain sensitive to the movements of the Spirit, since he cannot be absolutely sure of what belongs to the treasure of faith and of what is part of the earthen vessel containing it. He must avoid substituting for the Gospel of Christ the gospel of his own 'particular coterie'. In his attitude to other religions and ideologies he should draw a line between the message entrusted by God to man and all the philosophical, political, cultural and religious 'isms', which might blurr the uniqueness of Christ. It is the responsibility of a Christian to bring the Gospel of the 'full Christ' to light. This is the answer to the problem of inclusiveness and exclusiveness. Indeed it is the answer to the problem of wholeness. Visser't Hooft affirms very strongly that "If we do not 'preach ourselves' but Christ, and the whole Christ, there is no real issue between the inclusive and the exclusive attitude. The gospel itself will take care of what should be included and what should be excluded. We are no longer dependent upon ourselves alone to make the choice. The light shines in the darkness and will clearly show up what is darkness and what is light. Christianity is exclusive in so far as Christ excludes. Our only hope of finding a way through the complexity of modern life is therefore to deepen our loyalty to Him, and to listen more attentively to the message which God gave us through Him."[28]

Jesus Christ does not teach a new philosophy. He acts as God's representative; he is the liberator of humanity. He forgives sins, which is a matter of scandal and astonishment to the world. But this is essential; for the ideal of the Gospel must enter into the realm of life. Christ is relevant only when he makes it possible for man to experience a relationship of reconciliation with God. The Gospel of incarnation enters into the realm of facts in the death of Christ on the Cross. This is the sacrifice through which the Kingdom is ushered in. Man is reunited with God; he is made whole. "This whole emphasis on sin and grace is then not merely a theological invention. It is rather the characteristic that distinguishes a Christianity which has come to grips with reality from a purely ideal Christianity 'in the air'. Without this emphasis, the Gospel is mere good advice without power. With this emphasis, it becomes a force of renewal and transformation."[29]

This may be a concept which has estranged many people from Christianity. Man is reluctant to place his center of gravity outside himself. The concept of the 'new creation' is absolutely foreign to him; and he does not see it exemplified in the lives of most Christians. He fails to see a complete transformation of life. He does not understand the eschatological dimension of that spiritual phenomenon, the fact that it is in hope and in faith that the Christian is already a new creature. Of course there is a danger of confusion today. It is created by those who look at the Gospel of 'spiritual freedom' as a way to escape the problem of ethics. Certainly we can no longer think of the Gospel merely in terms of principles and laws. That the Bible be more than a code of Law does not mean, however, that we are excused from all ethical decision. Unfortunately, Christians themselves have contributed to the impression that allegiance to any moral system is not essential to Christianity. Indeed, Christian morals have become out of date because they were too often only a morality instead of being the expression of a life hidden in God. Christian morals have lost their basis of conviction and faith and thus become meaningless. In a quest for renewal and wholeness, our task, therefore "is not to restore worn-out moral convictions but to produce men who have their address in God."[30] Visser't Hooft expresses himself quite clearly on that matter: "It may be that the particular standards and norms in which Christianity has expressed itself are becoming a matter of the past. Why not? They have no claim to eternal value. Christianity does not stand or fall with a particular code of behaviour, but with a particular relation to God which expresses itself in many diverse ways. Of those who would hold on to the established morals at all costs we may say what Jesus said to the Parisees: 'They make the word of God void by their tradition.' For Christian morality shares with all other Christian possessions the fate of being a 'treasure in earthen vessels.' The vessels may break and there is no reason to regret them. But the treasure remains. It alone is eternal because it is the Word of God. Puritanism, Victorianism, and a good many other--'isms' have their time and pass away.

But God remains a living God Who speaks to each time and generation. For the Christian the real struggle is never one of different systems of morals. It is rather one of different sources of morals. For him the question is not 'What shall we do?' but 'Whom shall we obey?'"[31]

The will of God is part of his revelation; and man's life must be set in the light of the whole history of salvation--"the whole history of God with men."[32]

Christians are called to serve God in the world, to share in the "cosmic task"[33] of Jesus Christ. In the light of the Reformation, Visser't Hooft insists that all Christian activity is the exercise of the Christian calling, not merely the 'religious activity.' "The essential thing is that the service we render in the world should not be detached from the service we render to God. The Christian calling is characterised by a certain asceticism. It does not look on the world as its prey. It witnesses to the reality of the other world which is promised to us, and in the light of which this world seems to be as it were a provisional and fallen world. The Christian lives in it, as a stranger. But he is a stranger who does not leave the world, who rather takes his place in it to attack it from within. For that is where, for the moment the great conflict must take place."[34]

This conflict will continue until such a time when the Kingdom of Christ is perfectly established. Christians, however, must collaborate with the world; but their collaboration "will never become an 'ideological' collaboration which sets revealed truth on the same plane as human truths,"[35] Visser't Hooft speaks of a collaboration "<u>ad hoc</u>,"[36] helping the world to seek the signs of God's justice but remaining aware that "the only true change for which we can hope must be brought by the Holy Spirit and will announce the complete renewal of heaven and of earth."[37]

It is the responsibility of the Christian, for example, to develop a conception to the state, of war and peace, of economics, of sex and of many other aspects of life in the light of his relationship to God. In some measure, he will be able to work out those problems within the common thought of the Christian community. Not completely, however; the Christian must learn to depend constantly upon the gift of grace and upon Christ, the Giver. This shows the two dimensions of 'wholeness'. "A Christian is then characterized, not only by the decision to follow Christ, but also by the decision to accept the renewal of life which Christ offers."[38]

Christian wholeness means living with God, in the presence of a divine, personal will; and not in a "mere confrontation with immutable and static principles or ideas."[39] It is in the hearing of God's call to obedience that man is being re-created, renewed, made whole. We receive that call and respond to it in an act of faith in Christ. Visser't Hooft says that: "faith is the ever-repeated acceptance of that offer and its realization in action."[40] Jesus Christ is the only possibility and expression of our encounter with God. In Christ, God communicates Himself to man and receives man unto Himself. In Christ eternity enters into time. This is the meaning of the incarnation. God breaks through our human limitations; salvation becomes a reality, a true dimension of our human condition. This does not mean that in the incarnation the historical personality of Jesus takes the place of God. Visser't Hooft stresses that "we are not to become disciples of a Jesus apart from God."[41] Life has no other center but God; and Christ Himself apart from God is completely distorted, the human half of the picture is exalted at the expense of the divine. In the historical reality of the incarnation, God is in Christ. "A Jesus who is only an improved edition of ourselves can inspire us, but He cannot make the real difference between the prison of self centeredness and transitoriness and the freedom of life with God. The Christian Church stands or falls with this simple proposition, that Jesus is nothing less than God's self-communication to man, and the only certain source of our knowledge of God."[42]

To believe is "the stuff of Christian Life."[43] Although there is no proof satisfactory to reason, Jesus Christ, as known in Scriptures, is truly the revealer of God. Faith is a matter of decision and commitment. Visser't Hooft would say that the truth of Christianity "is always of the nature of truth-to-live-by,"[44] not truth of the realm of science in the proper sense of that word. In other words the believer accepts the authority which the Bible claims when it speaks of Jesus Christ--the authority of the witness of God's specific revelation. To the ultimate question: 'Has God spoken to man, the Church and the world?' we answer 'He has in Jesus Christ.' "In Him God comes to us as the personal God, Who claims our lives, Who offers Himself as the one goal of life, giving meaning to our small existences. Do we believe in a personal God? We do because we have heard the word that He has spoken to us in His son. A God, Who loves us like that, cannot be less than personal."[45]

Finally, to find wholeness the Christian must receive the gift of Christ in the communion of his 'Body' or 'fellowship'. It is in and through the Church that God is calling him. It is the Church which God has entrusted with the passing on of the Gospel. As Secretary of the World's Student Christian Federation, Visser't Hooft has endeavoured to promote a "Church-ward."[46] movements among students. He has challenged them to take their stand for Christ in the actual churches; and he has warned them against "the pharisaical attitude of intellectual spectatorship."[47] He knew that there is no Christian wholeness outside the Church. In 1932, he wrote: "If Christian students today are increasingly willing to take the Church seriously it is that they begin to rediscover a very simple truth, which belongs to the essence of Christian faith, namely that God does not speak in generalities but in very specific terms. There is a particular place in history where God has revealed Himself: Jesus Christ. There is a particular place in the world where we hear His word spoken to us: the Church."[48]

This does not mean that the Church can make an ultimate decision for the individual Christian. The decision for or against God--prerequisite to the problem of wholeness--is the responsibility of each man. This is true also of the subsequent decisions as to what is the Will of God for the individual in the realm of ethics. All our decisions, however, are taken not in isolation but as members of a community. We are guided and strengthened by the Church. Indeed, the Christian has a need of and a right to receive from the Church a prophetic leadership. He must demand it and protest against the Church that refuses to give it. The only thing a Christian cannot do is cut himself away from the Church, even when it fails to be 'the Bride of Christ.' There is no renewal nor wholeness apart from the Church. Visser't Hooft writes what could be regarded as a statement on his relationship to the Church: "It is indeed a hard task to hold on to the visible church as in any sense the corollary of the invisible Church. But it must be done; for it is into this visible church with all its scandalous and dull characteristics that God calls us, and it is to it that He has entrusted the passing on of His good news. In these circumstances, our first task is to enter into this Church, and so to demonstrate that we want to be concrete Christians and not merely idea-Christians, but our second task is to fight for the Church against the Churches, to protest in the name of the Christian Community against the caricatures of the Christian Community. If we protested from some secure place outside the Church, we should become Pharisees; but if we enter into its ranks, live and toil with it and then protest against ourselves as well as against others, we may help to build the true Church, which will certainly be far from perfect, but which may at least be conscious of its own particular mission."49

As we are confronted by Christ and respond to Him, so must we be confronted by the Church and take it seriously. There again, ubi Christus, ibi Ecclesia. Wholeness in Christ is related to the question of the wholeness of the Church.

The Wholeness of the Church

We have seen how according to Visser't Hooft a divided Church is weak; for it has no clear, effective answer to the pressing questions of the world. Actually the Church is so weak that "it cannot defend itself against direct or indirect attacks be secular or idolatrous communities, except by affirming and demonstrating its own reality."

Such demonstration will become possible only when the Church,

renewed and united, will be transparent to God's action in Jesus
Christ. Then it will show its strength and wholeness. Visser't
Hooft does not see the wholeness of the Church as a vision of
the future only. Time and again in history the Church was renewed; and today more than ever it is already united in the preaching of the universal Kingship of Christ and brotherhood of man.
Indeed, the Church has demonstrated a great strength; and the
world by sharing in it would find in its own wholeness--a wholeness which cannot be conceived nor achieved apart from the wholeness of the Church. For Visser't Hooft the relation is clear:
the strength and wholeness of the Church are in Christ, whose
dominion reaches the full extent of the world. The weakness
of the Church--'the Church of the not-yet'--comes from its
inevitable association with the world; its strength comes from
its complete dependence upon God. Speaking of that strength of
the Church, Visser't Hooft says "[the Church] is strong in that
it does not depend on natural or human realities, but on God's
action in Jesus Christ. It cannot be broken by events in this
world, however tragic they may be, and however deeply they may
separate groups from each other. It goes through resurrection
after resurrection in the course of history, and continues to
live while all other communities great or small disappear. It
is strong also in that it does not depend on negation of or opposition to other communities, but cuts across all other communities and transcends them all. It is strong in its knowledge

that the decisive question for man is the question put to him
by God and not the questions put by the political and social
schemes through which men would save themselves. It is strong
in its realistic recognition that 'within the four seas all men
are not brothers', and in its no less realistic faith that in
and through Jesus Christ they can become brothers. And so it
impinges again and again on political and social reality, challenging the egocentrism of the natural communities, pointing beyond them to a greater and less exclusive fellowship, and sending its ambassadors into the natural communities with a ministry
of reconciliation and peace. It shares in the weakness of its
Lord who came into the world in the form of a Servant, and who
died on a Cross. It shares in the strength of its Lord who was
and is Lord, that is the beginning, the centre and the goal of
history."[51]

Hence, the real Church is a strong Church; the problem for
man and the world is to recognize the reality of the Church. How
can the Church's wholeness be visible?[52] Visser't Hooft suggests that the Christian task should start at home. "Christendom must be Christianized."[53] New forms of community are being
experimented in the world; some are already well established.
They all develop, however, outside the Christian Community. The
reason is that we have no real Community, no real Church. The
sense of the essential togetherness, oneness, and wholeness of

the Church has been lost, because of an individualistic concept of salvation.[54] The Church has become an appendix to the Christian life. Christians must help the world rediscover the Church as a community. Visser't Hooft suggests that materialism has led the world to a deadlock; men seek new foundations for their social life.[55] This could be, therefore, a time of opportunity for the real Church. To live up to that challenge, however, we must understand that in the true <u>ecclesia</u> "the Christian calling and the Christian Community are two aspects of the same reality."[56] Indeed, rediscovering the sense of Christian togetherness is the way to salvation and wholeness for the Church and the world. Visser't Hooft writes: "It is only when Christians discover that their faith is a community-building faith, and when the community-builders discover that true human community can be based only on faith in a super human community, that we may hope to get out of our present chaos."[57]

The world may reject that 'super human community', or it may refuse to recognize it; but the authenticity of the Church cannot be measured by its success or influence. Indeed, we have seen how a successful Church may be used by the state to political ends. In 1940, at the beginning of the war, Visser't Hooft could not help seeing the deep gulf being created in Nazi-dominated Europe between the Church and the new order. Rejecting pessimism, however, he had enough faith to write: "The real issue is then not, whether the world is willing to make a place for the Church, but rather, whether the Church is the Church, both in its own life and in relation to the world. The real issue is not whether the outward conditions justify an optimistic or pessimistic conclusion about the future of the Church, but rather, whether the Church lives by that life which is truly its own. The worst conditions cannot kill a living Church. The best conditions cannot resuscitate a dead Church. The Church should, therefore, not be obsessed by the reactions of the world. The great choice which it has to make is not between success or failure according to the standards of the world. The great choice is between obedience and disobedience. A historical moment, such as the one in which we live, may be a great warning and a sign which underlines the necessity of the choice. But the choice itself is a matter, not between the Church and the world, but between the Church and its Lord."[58]

If the Church is not truly a Christian Community it is not because of external adverse circumstances; it is because Christians do not believe sufficiently in Jesus Christ. They do not fully acknowledge His Kingship and do not let Him rule the Church.[59] Many Churches call themselves Christian, while being divided in their allegiance. They serve two masters: God and the nation, the Gospel and the established order, Christ and progress. It is not that the Church should deny all existing tension between its nature and mission, and the world. But when the tension turns into a conflict, the stand of the real Church ought to be clear. Visser't Hooft comments: "... the choice which the Church has to make between an umcompromising stand on its true foundation and a dualistic position of a double loyalty, partly to God and to other 'values', is indeed a choice between life and death."[60]

Visser't Hooft does not hesitate to speak of the "totalitarian claim of Christ" as necessary to the restoration and wholeness of the Christian Community. He defines as follows the totalitarianism of Christ: "Totalitarianism implies two convictions: first that all of life is to be dominated by one ultimate reality and secondly, that this ultimate realtiy depends for its validity, not on the subjective judgment of the individual but on its own objective truth. A truly Christian Community is, therefore a body of persons who do not merely add Christ on to the other 'values' which they have discovered, but who make him the center of reference, who feel bound to him and let themselves to be judged and led by him."[61]

This concern for uniqueness and wholeness may qualify the openess of the Church to the world; it does not deny it. The renewed Church, which has rediscovered itself and learned again the meaning of Community, is ready to re-affirm its universality. It can demonstrate to the world an all-comprehensive love in the face of the divisive forces of race, class, and nation. In the time of God's choosing, when the Church becomes truly a worldwide body--no longer identical to any particular tradition or organization--the unity of the Christian community will usher in the unity of a World community. Is this only a dream? Visser't Hooft refuses to speak as a prophet. But in the darkest hours of the war he was already thinking of reconstruction, reconciliation and unity: "We do not know whether it is God's plan that anything like a world order may arise out of the present chaos. But we do know that it cannot come in any other way than by the growth of centres of order, groups and communities of men and women who live ordered lives in togetherness. To create such centres of order, to give new meaning to whatever remains of God's order in our society, and to create that order where chaos reigns today, is a slow and difficult task. It can only be undertaken by those who learn patience from the patience of God and who learn not to be obsessed by things seen, but to have faith in things not seen."[62]

In the present situation, as unity still lies in the future, the Church owes it to the world to speak a 'prophetic' word. It must be again the salt of the earth. We have seen that such a message, to have authority, should be spoken in confrontation with God's Word. Furthermore, it should be concrete; that is, it should be related to a given historical situation.[63] The prophetic word of the Church should inspire all Christian laymen and incite them to enter the political arena and work for the wholeness of society as members of the Christian Church. "As a Christian Community it [the Church] should give to its members the materials, the basic insights and convictions with which they can arrive at Christian decisions. As a Christian Community it should enable them to be in constant intimate touch with representatives of classes, races and nations other than their own, and thus help them to overcome their group-egotism."[64]

The Church exists for the sake of God's work in the world. It must share in the common burden of mankind. This is the responsibility of the common calling of the Church; and it is at this point that the Church faces today a great need for renewal. This is where the Church must choose and accept the consequences of standing for God. "The Church has, therefore, to care desperately for the salvation of the world and dare not leave that world to its fate. To refuse to listen to the voice of strangers does not mean to refuse to listen to mankind in need. For it is Christ Himself whom we serve in serving our fellow-beings. The Church must then feel profoundly concerned with maintaining that order in society which makes it possible to witness to the Gospel and to live the Christian life in all respects."[65]

This concern points our attention to the true meaning of catholicity, when the Church is striving to show forth the fullness of Christ's sovereignty. It points also to the ultimate dimension of wholeness, when the restoration of the Church leads to the healing of the world, when the Church denies itself for the sake of mankind. The wholeness of the Church is visible in reconciliation, when the community of man becomes one under God. Visser't Hooft suggests that the history of the movements of renewal during the last three centuries has precisely been used by God to bring about a real measure of unity and wholeness in the life of the Church. The redeeming power of Christ is constantly at work, building the Churches into one People of God. With great conviction, he remarks: "In spite of our isolationism and self-centeredness God has nevertheless continued to build the Church of Christ. He has broken through our divisions and dealt with His Church as a whole. As one looks closely at the story of the Church one not only sees how Churches live unto themselves, one sees also that they are again and again brought into close spiritual relationship to each other. There is as it were an underground movement through which the economy of the charismata operates across the confessional or denominational barriers. And this becomes specially visible in the movements for the renewal of the Church. For a genuine renewal in any particular Church is never a merely local or regional affair. It must of necessity seek to penetrate into the life of other Churches. The Spirit is no respector of Churches. When renewal is given to one Church, it is given 'for the common good', for the whole Church of Christ. So we find that almost every moment for renewal in Church history has affected Churches other than the one in which it began."[66]

It is true that Visser't Hooft has always looked at the Church with hope and understanding. Once, he called the twentieth century "the century of the Church."[67] For him, the Church is always confronted with "open doors,"[68] although he recognizes that the great days of 'Christendom' are passed. He believes that the true Church exists in spite of the world. While listening to its critics, he is free to reject their judgments as "spiritually false" and "misleading in point of fact."[69] He thinks also that those who are pessimistic have not understood what the Church is. What he says about them could be applied to all critics of the Church: "They take their starting-point in the world and consider the Church merely as one of the many forces which together shape history. But in doing so, they neglect the fundamental fact about the Church, namely, that it is the Church of God. They have not grasped that, in order to understand the true situation of the Church in the world, one must begin with the Church itself and ask whether it fulfils truly its mission, which has not been entrusted to it by the world, but by its Lord."[70]

Is the Church today the true Church of Jesus Christ? Of

course the question is not simple; and Visser't Hooft has never attempted to answer it, at least not in moral terms. Theologically, however, he did not avoid it. Basing his ecclesiology upon the concept of the Kingship of Christ, he reaffirmed that the real Church exists, lives and toils in obedience to its Lord. His claim is that the Church is rediscovering the way of obedience; therefore, it is being renewed and slowly made whole. The Church becomes the Church. We let Visser't Hooft himself close this study on a note of sober, realistic but certain hope. It was written in 1940, when many people despaired of the Church. "Is the Church today truly the Church, and has it made up its mind that it must obey its Lord and not obey other lords and masters? One cannot give a simple affirmative answer to this question. The truth is, that the Church is only beginning to ask that question of itself. It is not altogether a sleeping Church, but neither is it altogether a Church that is wide awake. One might compare the Church today to an army at the moment of mobilization, but then an extremely chaotic and badly organized mobilization. Part of the troops are already in the front trenches and fight with remarkable courage; others prepare themselves seriously for the battle and are ready to leave at a moment's notice; others again discover suddenly that they are not sufficiently armed for a serious war and seek feverishly to procure what they need for the battle; but there are also those who have not heard the ringing of the bells, and who go on sleeping as if there were no war.

We should not be too astonished about the fact that the mobilization does not succeed too well. After all, the Church has lived for so long in an atmosphere of security that it finds it difficult to become accustomed to the notion that it will again have to fight for his very life. It was so comfortably settled in the human city that it has difficulty in adjusting itself to the adventurous life of Christian soldiers who have no abiding city. It was so bound to the world that it does not easily claim its full freedom of action. But the fact remains that there is a mobilization. Something is happening in the Church. Even if it is not yet the Church, it is becoming the Church. And that is already a very great reason for hope."[71]

CONCLUSION

CONCLUSION

The aim of this study has been to define the meaning of Church renewal in the thought of Visser't Hooft, and to see how in his view Church renewal and Church unity are integrally related.

Visser't Hooft begins with a realization of the failure of the historical Church to be the Church of Christ and to obey the only power which can offer man true freedom. The Church, according to Visser't Hooft, has not seen its relationship to Christ and to the world in the light of an absolute dependence upon God. It has broken away from the bibilical faith. Visser't Hooft's interpretation of Church history is that too often the Church has presumed to identify itself with Christ, thereby substituting the sovereignty of man for the sovereignty of God. Also, the Church has mistakenly regarded the Kingdom of God as its present possession, thus making difficult all possibility of renewal.

Certainly, the Church must be defined in terms of its relationship to the Kingdom. Visser't Hooft makes this point quite clear. He rejects all secular thinking about the Church. The Church, however, should resist the temptation of 'self-identification' with Christ and the Kingdom. It should see itself as existing between the times, between the 'already' and the 'not yet', in the eschatological reality of the Kingdom. In other words, for Visser't Hooft, the Church exists by virtue of its hope, dependent upon a fact in history; the resurrection of Christ.

'Christocentricity' is the controlling motif for Visser't Hooft's concept of renewal. In this respect, the second chapter of this study is certainly most important.

In Christ, Visser't Hooft discovers the 'concreteness' of God's activity in history. The humanity of Jesus Christ is the sign of such an activity. Visser't Hooft has a biblical view of history, interpreted as a history of salvation, progressing from Israel to the Church and from promise to fulfilment and centered in Jesus Christ. The decisive 'God-man' relationship is constituted in the 'Christic event' and that same event is constitutive of the faith of the Church--indeed, of its very life and of its hope for renewal, of its future.

Here, Visser't Hooft is definitely Barthian. He rejects all forms of natural theology. Apart from Jesus Christ, man can have no genuine knowledge of God, no experience of salvation. God alone, by grace, gives men a share in the event by which he reveals himself to the world. God's revelation in Jesus Christ has a character of perfection and finality which determines the nature of the relationship of the Church to its Master. The Church must find in Christ the meaning by which it understands itself, orders its life, and fulfills its mission. The same act of divine revelation determines also the relationship of the Church to the world. The ultimate meaning of history, before and after Christ, rests on the claim of faith that past and future converge in him. The 'Christic event' is already the consummation of history. Christ, therefore, exercises a divine Kingship over history, over the Church and the world. The Church is a witness; its mission is to proclaim this Kingship of Christ to the whole world, for God's action in history, in the life of the world, is now determined and conditioned by his decision to reveal himself to man in Jesus Christ.

For Visser't Hooft, a strong christology is necessary to establish and maintain the independence of the Christian message from other ideologies and theologies. Christology is more important today than ever before, suggests Visser't Hooft, since the Church has to live in a pluralistic milieu. The Christian society is no longer a reality; the Church cannot dream of the re-establishment of a Corpus Christianum, in which it occupies a 'monopolistic' position. Renewal and unity can be only a sign of Christ's presence in the life of the Church. It is Visser't Hooft's position that the Church must accept the fact of pluralism, but without renouncing the claim that the Gospel is universal and the Kingship of Christ cosmic. The Church must reject theological relativism as compromising the integrity of its prophetic mission. The question of renewal and unity cannot be isolated from the question of truth and wholeness. It is only by confessing the Kingship of Christ that the Church is renewed, for God's design of salvation is revealed in Jesus Christ. Hence, renewal is essentially a movement towards christocentricity. In the experience of renewal the Church moves from "ecclesiocracy" to "Christocracy." Visser't Hooft is convinced of two things: first, that the cosmic plan of salvation cannot be implemented outside the Church; the future belongs to the Church: "I am with you always to the close of the age." (Matt. 28:20), and second, that the Church itself cannot fulfill its mission unless it constantly remains under the judgment of its King. Christ is the true and only <u>via salutis</u>.

Visser't Hooft, therefore, views ecclesiology and the related problem of renewal and unity in the light of Christology. Like Barth, he insists that the whole world of man and the life of the Church must be seen in the light of the victory of Christ--a victory over sin and death which is the center of history, a present reality, yet still a coming event. In another Barthian note, Visser't Hooft stresses the eschatological dimension of the dominion of Christ and, consequently, of the nature of the Church. Existing between the time of reconciliation and of fulfillment, the crucial issue of renewal for the Church is to live as the subject and servant of a Kingdom still <u>in spe</u> and yet already <u>in re</u>. Because of this 'interim' characteristic of its being, the Church must continue to live in a situation of tension between conflicting concerns. The relation of the Church to the world, and more particularly to the state, is never an easy one. The Church belongs already to the 'new age'; the people of God is now reconciled to God and 'saved'. In the experience of salvation, however, the Church is confronting an unredeemed world, sometimes opposed to its mission. On the other hand, Christians and the Church live 'in the world' because they do not fully share in the life of a Kingdom yet to be perfected by the second coming of Christ. Hence, the temptation is for the Church of God to become the Church of man, to lose its identity and to betray its calling. The Church cannot abandon the world to its fate; but it should not forsake its own independence. The Church must speak to the world, not to itself, and in the name of God, not in its own name. Visser't Hooft compares the relations of the Church to the world with the movement of a "pendulum." He suggests that the Church should "enter into the world and withdraw out of the world by a process as rhythmical and as indispensable for its life as breathing is to human body."[1]

Having emphasized the eschatological dimension of the Kingship of Christ and of the Church's witness, Visser't Hooft defines the conditions and characteristics of renewal. His understanding of the way of renewal is informed by the history of Israel. He discovers there a pattern of history; he uses the term "cycle." The history of Israel is a movement progressing from alienation to reconciliation, from rebellion to self-surrender. Hence, renewal must begin with repentance--<u>metanoia</u>--. The Church has in Christ a high-priest able to sympathize with the weakness of his people and willing to renew its life. The message of renewal is part of God's revelation in Jesus Christ. This leads Visser't Hooft to say that renewal could be neither a human act, nor a structural reform. It is an intervention of the Holy Spirit bringing the Church back to its Lord. The way of renewal is obedience to the Spirit.

The Church, to be renewed must be constantly confronted with its Lord, recalled to obedience, re-orientated towards the new age, and re-consecrated to its threefold calling: first, to be in Christ, second, to make the manifestation of God in history known to all men, and third, to serve the world under the sign of the cross, to witness to a new order in the life of the old creation. Finally, to be renewed, the Church must see itself in the light of God. God sees His Church as a 'whole,' despite its divisions. Renewal and unity are steps forward for the manifestation of the wholeness of the Church. Visser't Hooft insists that in the corporate reality of the Church, the wholeness, of the individual Christian conditions that of the community.

Wholeness is essentially, for Visser't Hooft, a matter of

choice for or against God. Here again, we can detect a Barthian influence. Man and the Church must cease to defy God; they must renounce their pride and presumption. They must accept the fact that faith necessarily illustrates the contradiction between God and the world. The opposition of God and man should incite the latter to adopt an attitude of humility and dependence. Visser't Hooft has a high sense of the transcendence of God. To choose for God is to choose for Christ. It is a choice of faith between the truth of Christianity revealed in Jesus Christ and the truth of other religious traditions. There is no wholeness in relativism, which looks upon the content of faith as secondary and reduces Christianity to a system of ethics. The crucial issue of wholeness ultimately is not to resolve whether God exists but whether he is personal. In other words, we have returned where we started, namely to the truth that Christianity is centered around the event of the incarnation. Christ is relevant only when He gives wholeness to man, when He makes it possible for him to experience a relationship of reconciliation with God. Hence, Christian wholeness means living with God and for man, in the presence of a divine, personal will.

In the same manner, the strength and wholeness of the Church are in Christ. Wholeness, however, is a tangible phenomenon, a visible and corporate reality. It is the sign of the true Koinonia. The Church must rediscover this sense of Christian togetherness. The concepts of wholeness and uniqueness are inter-related. Living in a situation of tension and conflict, the Church cannot compromise its loyalty to Christ nor its prophetic mission. And yet, the Church must demonstrate to the world an all-comprehensive love.

In his work, Visser't Hooft has pleaded for what may be called a rediscovery of the Church. He feels deeply that the historical churches will never come together in a constructive movement of unity, unless they abandon what he calls "secular thinking about the Church."[2] The Christian churches must confess that "the Church by its very nature belongs to God and that in its message and method it dares not follow the ways of the world, but must constantly seek to discover His mind, His will."[3] The Church of Christ exists; for Visser't Hooft, it is a great objective fact, as well as a reality of faith and hope. The essence and the task of the ecumenical movement is to manifest the Church in its wholeness.

The quest for the true Church of Jesus Christ has been Visser't Hooft's constant preoccupation. Both as a churchman and as a theologian he has always stressed, with profound theological insight and great 'force', the importance of authenticity for the future of the Church.

It has been suggested that Visser't Hooft came to deeply

under the influence of Karl Barth and that his theology is too "continental."[4] It has also been said that his "dogmatism" has made him unsympathetic to some.[5] There may be substance in these criticisms, but we should note that historically, at least during three decades, Neo-Orthodoxy had become in Europe a kind of theological *lingua franca* which certainly helped more than hindered ecumenical encounters. More important, however, is the fact that Visser't Hooft was moved by deep convictions, based on ideas as true to him as they were to Barth. The Church can never be the source of its own renewal. Christ alone is the hope of the Church. To be renewed and reformed in unity, the Church must be given a form which expresses the truth that Jesus Christ is its King.

END NOTES

INTRODUCTION

1. The Sufficiency of God, edited by Robert C. Mackie and Charles C. West (London: S.C.M. Press, 1963).

2. Ibid., p. 15.

3. Suzanne de Dietrich, The Sufficiency of God, "Crisis and Renewal in the Student World," p. 36.

4. W. A. Visser't Hooft, Memoirs, (London: S.C.M. Press, 1973).

5. Visser't Hooft is predominantly a lecturer and an editorialist. Most of his work is found in periodicals, and many of his books are compiled lectures. The fact that in most cases he does not give exact documentation indicates in some measure the nature of his work and the conditions under which he wrote. For example, in 1937 he wrote a book entitled Non Other Gods which contains neither footnotes not bibliography. It is thus sometimes difficult to trace the sources of his thought.

CHAPTER I

1. "L'Eglise à la croisée des chemins" Cahiers Protestants XXIV, 3 (1940) p. 146.
2. "Christianity as its own Adversary" S.W., XXXI, 2 (1938), p. 101.
3. "After a Year of Message Study," S.W., XXIV, 2 (1931), p. 101.
4. "Prefaced or Epilogue," S.W., XXIV, 3 (1931), pp. 187-188.
5. S.W., XXIV, 3 (1931), p. 102.
6. Daniel Jenkins Beyond Religion, (London: S.C.M. Press, 1962), p. 28.
7. S.W., XXI, 2 (1939), p. 102.
8. S.W., XXVI, 2 (1938), pp. 115-125.
Article for which Visser't Hooft wrote the introduction and editorial: "Christianity as its own Adversary."
9. Ibid., pp. 119-120.
Visser't Hooft remarks that in the first case the Church became the voice of a dying bourgeoisie and in the second case it failed to be a real 'vis-a-vis' of the State: Pendant longtemps elle avait oublié qu'il appartient a sa mission d'être un veritable vis-a-vis de l'Etat. Et ce n'est qui lentement et à travers de grands judements qu'elle apprend ce que c'est que d'agir en sentinelle de Dieu. Sa vocation à l'égard de l'Etat est de lui rappeler, constamment, les limites d'en-haut, comme le peuple lui rappelle les limites d'en bas. Les limites d'en haut, c'est-a-dire les frontières entre l'Etat veritable, qui est serviteur de Dieu, et l'Etat qui s'adore lui-meme et tombe sous le jugement porté sur ceux qui se mettent à la place de Dieu. L'Eglise aura donc à dire à l'Etat que l'homme n'existe pas pour son bon plairsir; qu'il est soumis à des critères de justice qu'il n'est pas dans son pouvoir d'affaiblir ou de changer. Et elle le lui dira concrètement chaque fois qu'elle constatera un glissement vers l'idolatrie totalitaire.

L'Eglise n'est pas considérée comme le porte-parole d'un message de salut cosmique et comme sentinelle du Dieu juste qui protège les pauvres. Elle est encore considérée comme une voix de la bourgeoisie mourante, qui defend ses intérêts sous le comouflage de grands slogans chrétiens. Ne semble-t-il pas qu' elle est tougours du côté de l'ordre politique plurôt que de la justice sociale? Ne defend-elle pas la propriété privée sans toutefois s'attaquer aux abus de cette propriete privee tout de même si chairement dénoncés dans la Bible? "L'Eglise et la mission actuelle de l'Europe", Cahiers des Associations Professionnelles Protestants, 3-4-5 (1945) pp. 44-45.
10. Indeed, the Christian Theologian is the only one equal to the task of criticizing the Church, for he alone can see it from the inside. Cf "L'Eglise à la croisee des Chemins" Cahiers

Protestants XXIV, 3 (1940) p. 140.
  11. S.W., XXXII, 3 and 4 (1940), pp. 195-205.
  12. S.W., XXVI, 2 (1938), p. 118.
  13. The Documents of Vatican II, ed. Walter M. Abbott, trans., ed. Joseph Gallagher (New York: Guild Press, 1956), c.5, p. 39.
  14. The Renewal of the Church (Philadelphia: The Westminister Press, 1956), p. 37.

In another article, published earlier, in 1940, Visser't Hooft had remarked that a lack of concern for renewal can be a sign of spiritual unfaithfulness. An unfaithful Church is either asleep or unaware of its unique mission before God. In some cases it can be a church consciously serving false gods. The three characteristics of an unfaithful church are: first, the unfaithful Church does not repent; second, the unfaithful Church adjusts to the world or finds refuge in otherworldliness; third, an unfaithful Church denies the reality of the Universal Church.

a) L'Eglise infidèle ne se repent pas.

Elle parle à Dieu comme si elle avait le droit de lui reclamer des privileges. Elle revendique ses droits devant Dieu. Elle trouve que Dieu doit nous aider dans notre misère, que les chrétiens ont droit a tout ce qu'ils possedent, a une certaine sécurité, a un certain standard de vie, a être protégés contre le malheur. Au fond, c'est une Eglise qui prie comme les paiens. Le type de la prière paienne, c'est la priere magique qui veut forcer la volonté et le secours divins.

Or, n'est-ce pas paien de prier seulement lorsque l'eau monte, que notre sécurité est menacée? On parle d'un retour à l'Eglise. Parmi ceux qui y reviennent, il y en a qui ont vraiment compris qu'il faut se remettre entre les mains de Dieu, mais il y a aussi cet effort magique pour forcer Dieu à venir à l'aide.

b) L'Eglise infidèle s'adapte au monde ou se refugie dans l'au-dela.

L'Eglise infidèle s'adapte continuellement. Elle "se laisse emporter à tout vent de doctrine." Dans un pays, elle prêche une chose, dans un autre pays une autre chose. En temps de paix, elle est pacifiste; en temps de guerre, elle est militariste. Elle ne se laisse pas guider par l'Esprit, mais par tous les esprits.

Ou bien, son infidelité consiste en ceci, qu'elle devient si spirituelle qu'elle n'a plus rien a voir avec le monde. Elle n'enseigne plus que et qui est eternel et se désintéresse de ce qui se passe sur la terre. Elle oublie que Jesus-Christ est venu, a souffert, sur cette terre, que la Croix a été dressée dans l'histoire.

La question est justement de savoir s'il y aura obeissance

à Dieu sur cette terre. L'Eglise "du ciel" est moins spirituelle qu'elle ne le pense; elle est infidele parce qu'elle n'accepte pas la mission difficile et plus immediate que Dieu lui a adressee. Elle joue le jeu des pires adversaires de l'Eglise (Rosenberg, Goebbels, n'ont rien a reprocher a cette Eglise, puis qu' elle ne se mêle de rien).
c) L'Eglise infidele nie la realité de l'église universelle.

Or, dans ce domaine aussi, il y a beaucoup de signes d' infidelite dans not Eglises. Quand on lit les journaux religieux de nos differents pays, qu'on entend des sermons, discerne-t-on reellement que, parmi nous, "quand un membre souffre, tous les autres membres souffrent avec lui?"

N'avons-nous pas négligé la promesse qui contient aussi un commandement: "Que tous soient un?" Avons-nous assez prié pour nos frères de Russie, d'Allemagne et de tant d'autres Eglises qui souffrent?

Ne prenons-nous pas trop au serieux les frontieres politiques et geographiques, qui n'ont rien a voir avec la réalité de notre unite en Christ par-dessus toutes frontieres? N'acceptons-nous, membres du Corps de Christ?
L'Eglise devant les événements Tirage a part du "Messager" de l'Eglise evangelique libre de Geneve. (1940) pp. 4-5.

15. Speaking of religion in general, K.S. Latourette remarks: "... evidence of the continuing vitality of a religion seems to be in what looks like contradictory manifestations. On the one hand are the incorporation of elements from different cultures and changing climates of opinion and stimulus to individuals and groups to initiate fresh movements with drastic modifications and innovations. On the other hand there is the persistence of distinguishing prime characteristics which are never fully relinquished. Unless it has both these qualities, a religion has neither a wide spread nor a long life."
Challenge and Conformity, "Studies in the interaction of Christianity and the world of today," (New York: Harper and Bro., 1955), p. 16.

16. W.A. Visser't Hooft and J.H. Oldham, The Church and its Function in Society (London: George Allen and Unwin Ltd, 1937), p. 59. Visser't Hooft wrote part II of the book. It is entitled "The Church and the Churches."

17. Renewal, pp. 69-70.

18. We should not, however, overdramatize the overrunning power of the barbarian invasions, wiping out, so to speak, the Latin civilization of Western Europe. Temptation to 'romanticism' has been very strong in the past. Timothy M. Parker, in his 1955 Bampton Lectures, stresses the social and economic reasons which accelerated the process of disintegration of the Roman Empire, and the emergence of a new society organized into independent

Kingdoms, Christian if not orthodox, under barbarian Kings. Parker suggests that the idea of Empire could easily be revived by Charlemagne because, in fact, it had never been lost in the West: "... every Western State, be it as barbarised as one pleases to think -- and none was wholly barbarian -- thought of itself as in a sense a microcosm of the old Empire." Christianity and State in the Light of History (London: Adam and Charles Black, 1955), p. 97.

19. Charlemagne, in fact, regarded it as his function and responsibility to rule the Church as well as the State. He was more than the Protector of the Church; he looked upon his office as that of defender of the faith as indicates the role he played at the Council of Frankfort in 794, summoned by his order. See T.M. Parker, Christianity and State, c. 5, p. 93.

20. Church and its Function, pp. 60-61.

21. "The Church and Europe," S.W., XXXII, 3 & 4 (1940), p. 196.

Almost twenty years later, in 1959, Visser't Hooft, reflecting on the development of the "dialogue eccuménique" since 1910, gives to that period of marriage between Church and State in the history of Europe the name of "L'ère constantinienne."

L'ère constantinienne debuta lorsque l'empereur Constantin prit l'Eglise sous sa protection; elle connut son age d'or dans la communauté chretienne du Moyen Age; elle était basée sur l'idée que (selon les termes de Richard Hooker) "dans un Etat ou un Royaume chretien, un seul et même peuple est l'Eglise et la communauté." Cette notion fut generalement maintenue jusqu'au 18 siecle. Alors apparurent des conceptions nouvelles de l'Eglise et de l'Etat; celui-ci se secularisa de plus en plus et les Eglises en de nombreuses contrées s'organisèrent en Eglises libres ou en Eglises nationales independantes.
"Importance des Eglise d'Asie dans le mouvement ecumenique," Eglise Vivante, Paris, Louvain 1939) XI, 6, pp. 423-424.

22. S.W., XXXII, 3 & 4 (1940), p. 197.

23. Christianity in a Revolutionary Age, I, "The Nineteenth Century in Europe - Background and the Roman Catholic Phase" (New York: Harper & Brothers, 1958), c. 7, p. 17.

24. In 1959 in the article mentioned one page earlier Visser't Hooft makes a distinction between the marriage of Church and State, which had ended by the time of the 16th century Reformation, and the marriage between Church and Society, which in fact lasted much longer until such time when the cultural structures of 20th century Europe and America were finally transformed.

Mais d'autres facteurs compliquaient la situation. Tandis que le mariage entre l'Etat et l'Eglise tirait à sa fin, on ne ou entre le Christianisme et la civilisation. Les cadres culturels montrent souvent une ténacité remarquable. Et les cadres

culturels de l'Europe et de l'Amerique étaient ceux de la chrétienté, d'une civilisation qui en depit de toute sa variété, en depit de la désunion et de la faiblesse des Eglises chrétiennes, en depit des ideologies antireligieuses, vivait d'une ethique dérivée de la religion chrétienne. Ceci ne signifie pas qu'elle était un pur reflet de l'Evangile. Les civilisations ne sont jamais le pur reflet d'une religion. Cette chrétienté occidentale était le resultat de la rencontre du Christianisme avec les realities sociales, politiques, economiques, culturelles, de l'histoire européenne et américaine. Parfois, les mobiles chretiens avaient modelé cette ethique; parfois, des conditions historiques avaient déformé les mobiles chretiens. Inevitablement, le résultat était un compromis ou le bien et le mal, les valeurs permanentes et les ajustements transitoires se trouvaient étrangement mêlés.
"Importance des Eglises d'Asie dans le mouvement ecumenique." p. 424.
 25. S.W., XXXII, 3 & 4 (1940), p. 118.
 26. Church and its Function, p. 73.
 27. The Tridentine Church regarded renewal only as a structural readaptation and doctrinal re-formulation not as a returning of the whole Church to its Lord, although the urge for reform remained always alive in individuals of various persuasions and in minority groups. In the Catholic tradition all effort for renewal was defeated by the Tridentine assumption that the Church was the initiator, criterion and judge of its own renewal: "Trent by declaring that the traditions which had been dictated by the Holy Spirit and conserved in the Catholic Church through continuous succession were to be accepted and venerated 'with the same feeling of piety and reverence' as Holy Scripture, the Council said in fact that the Church is judge in its own cause and that its criterion of newness is not the new age, but the inherent law of its own life." Renewal, p. 76.
 Visser't Hooft remarks also that: "The story of the Roman Catholic Church since the Council of Trent is essentially the story of the increasingly uncompromising and explicit definition of the ecclesiological and sociological ideas which are implied in the medieval order." Church and its Function, p. 62.
 28. Locke's emphasis on the power of reason to resolve all problems of natural theology, namely the proof of the existence of a divine Being, not only depersonalized the concept of God but also questioned the necessity of Revelation, the role of which was simply to confirm the reasonable character of Christianity. Cf. Gerald R. Cragg, The Church and the Age of Reason, 1648-1789 (Baltimore: Penguin Books, 1966) pp. 65-80.
 29. Lord Herbert of Cherbury had summarized the Deistic doctrine in five fundamental truths: "God exists: it is our duty to worship him; the proper way to do so is to practice vir-

tue; men ought to repent of their sins; rewards and punishments will follow death." G.R. Cragg, Ibid., p. 77. Cf. John Dillenberger and Claude Welsh, Protestant Christianity interpreted through its Development (New York: Charles Scribner's Sons, 1954), pp. 156-159.
    30. Church and its Function, pp. 73-74.
    31. Church and its Function, p. 73.
    32. Alec R. Vilder remarks that it was in France that the question regarding the fate of the Church was answered most strikingly: "... it is in France that the political impact of the age of revolution upon the Church can best be studied. Not that any stable solution was arrived at there, either in the years succeeding 1789 or at any subsequent time. Rather, it is the variety, the fluctuations, and the instability of the relations between Church, State, and Society since 1789 that make French ecclesiastical histroy a paradigm both of the insecurity and of a survival of Christianity in this age." The Church in an Age of Revolution (Baltimore: Penguin Books, 1965), pp. 11-12.
    33. Church and its Function, p. 74.
    34. Visser't Hooft has understood very well the importance of Thomism for the defense of the Catholic system and the effort of the Roman Catholic Church to preserve it: "The comprehensive system of Thomism is thus not only the formulation of the guiding ideals of medieval culture, but also the explanation ond justification of a particular experiment in building a Christian order [...], through the official sanction given to Thomism, it is today more than ever the normative conception of the Christian society." Church and its Function, p. 61.
    35. A.R. Vilder remarks that in consequence of the negative attitude of the Papacy from Pius IX's Syllabus Errorum of 1864--and Vatican I--to the death of Pius X in 1914, "... a promising renaissance of Catholic scholarship, especially biblical scholarship, was set back for more than a generation. [...] This setback for Catholic scholarship, especially for critical and objective study of Christian origins, was then one consequence of the nipping in the bud of the modernist movement and of its ruthless suppression." 20th Century Defenders of the Faith (London: S.C.M. Press, 1965), pp. 36-37.
    36. Church and its Function, p. 81.
Cf. also The Background of the Social Gospel in America (St. Louis: Bethany Press, 1966 Reprint), pp. 1-15.
    37. S.W. XXXII, 3 & 4 (1940), p. 199.
    38. Misère et grandeur de l'Eglise (Geneve: Labor et Fides - 1943) pp. 17 & 19. Those three pages, though very brief, are essential to grasp Visser't Hooft's understanding of twenty centuries of Church History: Grandeur et misère du nouveau peuple

"Et maintenant, le nouveau peuple va croître, Bientôt, il est devenu si fort que les puissances de ce monde doivent compter avec lui. Que va-t-on faire de ce peuple hors-cadre? Puisque les tentatives de l'exterminer ne font que le renforcer, les hommes d'Etat arrivent à la conclusion qu'il vaut mieux s'entendre avec lui. C'est pourquoi Constantin et ses successeurs offrent à l'Eglise un pacte d'amitié et de collaboration qui, selon lui, sera à l'avantage des deux parties. Attention, peuple de Dieu! Sera-ce vraiment à ton avantage? Ne deviendras-tu pas "comme les autres peuples?" Souviens-toi que ton histoire a commencé par un grand départ et que ton Dieu t'a fait sortir des pays ou tu voulais t'installer!

Mais l'attraction d'une vie tranquille est trope forte. Le peuple de Dieu se laisse apprivoiser. En theorie, il soumet les peuples. En fait, il y a penetration mutuelle. Tandis que Rome est christianisée, l'Eglise est romanisée. L'esprit de Rome, esprit du code legal et de l'institutionalisme, esprit tout à fait terrestre et tourné vers le présent, fait concurrence à l'Esprit Saint, Esprit libre et prophétique, Esprit éternel et tourné vers l'avenir de Dieu. Ainsi, le peuple de l'Eglise cesse d'être un peuple vraiment mouveau. Les anciens malentendus qui avaient déjà menacé le peuple d'Israel apparaissent encore une fois. Le peuple de Dieu se constitue comme les autres peuples. Il aura un chef "qui marchera à sa tête," qui cherchera à le dominer, oui, qui osera même réclamer le <u>dominium mundi</u>. Boniface VIII ose pretendre "que toute créature humaine est soumise au Pape de Rome."

Cette Eglise croit que sa situation privilégiée est éternelle, inaliénable. Ainsi l'histoire se répète. Les grands avertissements de Dieu au peuple d'Israel sont oubliés. Le peuple est de nouveau sur de son affaire. Il se vante de ses succès. Il ne sait plus que ces succès terrestres peuvent être inscrits comme des défaites dans les chroniques de Dieu. Et il oublie la distinction fondamentale: "Les rois des nations leur commandent en maitres. Pour vous, ne faites pas ainsi. Que celui qui gouverne parmi vous soit comme celui qui sert." (Luc 22:25-26.)

Oh! cette Eglise fait encore de grandes choses. Elle a au moins le sens d'être un peuple, de former une communauté qui transcende toutes divisions entre les hommes. Ainsi, elle est encore capable de dompter les peuples païens. Mais elle le fait de plus en plus selon les règles du monde, et elle cesse donc d'être le peuple <u>nouveau</u> dans le sens de la nouvelle creation.

Il faudra donc encore une fois une grande crise, un grand jugement divin, un grand depart. Les Reformateurs entendent le cri: "Sortez de Babylone" et partezt pour que le peuple soit reconstitué dans sa sainteté, dans sa nouveauté. Pendant un temps, il semble que la grande renaissance du peuple de Dieu est venue. Au XVIe siecle, il y a en Europe un peuple-Eglise qui est dans la vraie tradition de l'Israel de Dieu. Mais, malheureusement, une autre renaissance--celle-la de nature toute terrestre, toute concentrée sur l'autonomie de l'homme--est deja en train de conquerir le monde civilisé. Et, au lieu de la reconstitution de peuple de Dieu, on voit bientot la décadence generale du peuple. Aux XVIIIe et XIXe siècles, l'Eglise perd le sens de sa veritable mission historique et cosmique. Ce qui est grave, c'est que maintenant l'idée même du peuple de Dieu cesse d'être une vérité opérante. La religion devient une affaire privée. L'Eglise devient un centre de rassemblement pour les âmes qui cherchent leur salut d'une façon toute individuelle. Le peuple de Dieu cesse d'être un peuple, cesse d'avoir une identité reconnaissable et de former une communauté solide. Comparez l'effroyable doctrine: <u>cujus regio, ejus religio</u>--le prince décide de la religion de ses sujets--avec la conception d'une troisieme race! Mettez le protestant du XIXe siecle--avec son refrain: <u>mes</u> convictions religieuses et <u>ma</u> vie privée ne regardent personne--à côté du chretien de la communaute primitive qui se sent membre d'un corps visible aussi bien qu'invisible! Remarquez la contradiction entre ces Eglises divisées et atomisees qui s'ignorent ou se querellent--et le peuple uni en Christ, dans lequel la souffrance d'un seul membre fait souffrir tous les autres. Considerez la distance qui separe ces bourgeois, solidement installés dans ce monde, du peuple d'etrangers, de colons du Royaume de Dieu dont nous parle le Nouveau Testament!"

39. Visser't Hooft notes that it is the attitude of the world to reject the Church, while recognizing its past record. "For it is quite obvious that the Church has not been able to render the same services to Western civilization during the last centuries which it has been able to render to medieval Europe, or to Europe at the time of the Recivilization. It is no longer the spiritual leader of the nations. Today it finds itself outside the main currents which fashion the life of man. Modern man no longer seeks his moral nurture in the Church." The future of the Church is under discussion. Many claim that it is destined to disappear. The eventuality of a 'post-Christian world' cannot be dismissed too lightly. Here, Visser't Hooft voices his concern. "We are then forced to the conclusion that the great days of the Church are passed. It would seem that there is truth in the thesis of a recent German book with the significant title <u>Post Christum</u>, namely that we are at the end of the Christian era and are now entering into the post-Christian era in which Christianity will become merely a beautiful memory, and in which the relics of the Church, which may still survive, will become small sects which are either persecuted or, what is worse, simply forgotten." "The Task of the Christian Community Today,"

S.W., XXXIII, 1 (1940), pp. 76-77.
    40. S.W., XXXII, 3 & 4 (1940), pp. 201-202.
    41. "A Living Hope." The Cambridge Review LXXV, 1822 (1953) p. 150.
    42. Ibid.
    43. S.W. XXXII, 3 & 4 (1940), p. 203.
    44. Visser't Hooft has always been very concerned with the problem and has studied its nature and negative impact upon the life of the Church, as well as the heroic effort of the latter to maintain its independence. Many articles, editorials, diary-notes deal with the subject. See for example in the S.W.: "Is Facism a Religion?," "German Protestantism at the Cross Roads," "The Church in Germany," XXVI, 1 (1933) - XXVI, 3 (1933) - XXVII, 2 (1934).
    45. "A Living Hope." p. 149.
    46. S.W., XXXII, 3 & 4 (1940), p. 204.
    47. S.W., XXXII, 3 & 4 (1940), p. 205.
The same year, in the article already mentioned, Visser't Hooft elaborates on the theme of the faithful Church; a repentant Church assuming again a prophetic mission with a universal responsibility.

    C'est une Eglise reveillée, qui ne connait pas d'autre mission que d'obeir à la Parole de Dieu dont elle vit uniquement.
a) L'Eglise fidèle se repent.

    Elle sait se repentir (se repentir, c'est changer d'orientation spirituelle, c'est se tourner vers Dieu). Elle se rend compte que ce n'est pas seulement le monde, mais surtout l'Eglise qui a besoin de repentance. Car, avec toutes ses activités, avec toutes ses paroles, l'Eglise tournait le dos a Dieu. Et maintenant il est dit à l'Eglise: "Repens-toi." Ce qui se passe dans le monde est comme un immense appel à la repentance. Nous avons mérité tout cela, et plus encore. L'avons-nous vraiment compris: Ce n'est pas quelques petites fautes que nous avons a nous reprocher, c'est que continuellement nous nous détournons de Dieu. Nous nous appuyons sur mille choses du monde; nous comptons sur ces choses au fond de nous-mêmes. Ce sont à nos yeux des sécurités. Lorsque ces choses et que nous n'avons pas vraiment vécu par la foi.

    Voyez, par exemple, non pays, la Hollande, C'etait un pays calme, pas plus pécheur que les autres. On l'a considéré comme foncièrement chretien. Mais il y avait une satisfaction de soi profondement enracinée. En pratique, on y considerait certaines realités materielles aussi éternelles que la Parole de Dieu. Il y a avait un "bourgeois-satisfaitisme," on s'y était installé dans certains privilèges que l'on considerait comme très naturels

    Peut-être en est-il singulierement de même en Suisse. Un tel pays n'a-t-il pas besoin de ce grand choc? Ne devons-nous pas apprendre que le centre de l'Evangile est la Croix, qu'il faut souffrir pour suivre Jesus-Christ?

Il est terrible qu'il faille de telles leçons, de tels chocs pour nous purifier.

La repentance de l'Eglise est une chose terriblement actuelle. Toute l'issue de cette guerre dependra surtout de ceci: "Les chretiens sont-ils prêts à se repentir devant les évènements, ou ne sont-ils pas encore prêts? Si non, cela signifie qu'il faut encore une souffrance plus profonde.

Peut-être même la longueur de la guerre depend-elle de l'attitude des chrétiens. Se repentiront-ils? C'est de cette facon qu'il peuvent participer au plan de Dieu, hater la fin...

Cela ne veut pas dire que les chrétiens doivent passer leur temps a gémir. Car la repentance n'est pas une attitude passive. Elle est une <u>acceptation</u> sans recrimination de ce que Dieu ordonne; elle est aussi une nouvelle obeissance (les fruits de la repentance).

b) L'Eglise assume sa fonction prophetique.

La repentance ne doit donc pas rester une repentance generale. Elle doit nous amener aux decisions concrètes, à prendre position vis-a-vis des realites de l'heure. Nous ne sommes pas prophètes dans le sens de l'Ancien Testament. Toutefois, les Réformateurs n'ont pas eu tort quand ils parlaient de la fonction prophétique de l'Eglise: cette fonction implique que l'Eglise ne doit pas seulement proclamer la Parole de Dieu en général, mais encore amener ses membres à manifester leur obeissance dans leur vie quotidienne; non seulement la Parole qui touche les hommes de <u>ce temps-ci.</u>

Donc, il ne s'agit pas de s'évader, ce qui est notre grande tentation en temps de guerre. Il existe un spiritualisme chrétien qui rend la cité humaine aux ennemis de Dieu et devient ainsi, inconsciemment, le complice de Satan.

La guerre actuelle est, en effet, un curieux mélange d'une guerre politique avec une guerre spirituelle. Pour autant qu'il s'agit de guerre spirituelle, l'Eglise ne saurait rester neutre. La question delicate est de savoir ou finit la guerre spirituelle, et ou commence la guerre politique.

Quand, comme c'est le cas aujourd'hui, nous voyons dans l'action d'un des pays belligerants l'expression d'un esprit nettement anti-chretien (certes, les autres ne sont pas des anges), l'Eglise ne peut pas rester indifferente. C'est une affaire de conscience pour elle. Si l'Eglise n'a rien a dire contre les manifestations de cet esprit demoniaque, alors elle n'a plus de message pour ce monde, et elle joue le jeu de ces adversaires de l'Eglise qui proposent de laisser le monde aux politiciens et de renvoyer l'Eglise au ciel.

Il nous faut apprendre à resister spirituellement, ce qui est la resistance propre à l'Eglise. Savons-nous si nous n'aurons pas à lutter avec cet esprit dans nos propres Eglises, s' il n'y aura pas <u>ici</u> un conflit d'Eglise? Il faut se préparer pour savoir ce que l'Eglise devra dire lorsqu'elle sera confrontée avec cet esprit.

Certains faits montrent que cet esprit prophétique existe dans l'Eglise (Karl Barth, les Eglises des Etats-Unis, etc., ont osé parler).

Le Conseil oecumenique n'a pas pu parler puisqu'il n'a pas encore l'autorité pour une telle parole. Mais ses membres peuvent le faire individuellement, et beaucoup l'ont fait.

c) L'Eglise fidèle est consciente de faire partie de l"Eglise universelle.

Ce n'est pas du sentimentalisme. Il s'agit de compter avec le fait que Jésus a planté son Eglise partout dans le monde et que partout, il y a des frères.

Certes, il y a des séparations, du fait de la guerre. Des séparations mortelles, peut-être. Peut-on alors continuer de parler d'une Eglise universelle? Il le faut, car le Seigneur le veut.

Aujourd'hui encore, nous recevions des messages de chretiens d'Allemagne pour des officiers français sur le front. Je pense aussi à ces Chinois et ces Japonais qui, depuis trois ans, ont leur journée commune de prière, affirmant que dans la vraie prière, ils ne peuvent être séparés.

Certes, l'Eglise universelle n'est une réalité que pour peu de chrétiens. Mais elle peut le devenir pour tous. Cette realité ne peut être vraie que si elle est basée sur la vérité. Car la vraie unité ne sacrifie rien de la vérité.

Tout cela nous montre pourquoi il faut collaborer au Mouvement oecumenique. Certes, plusieurs pays ne le peuvent plus et nous ne savons pas si Dieu nous donnera l'occasion de continuer notre travail. Mais même si notre effort commun n'aboutit pas à la formation d'un Conseil oecumenique, il existe desormais une Eglise universelle. C'est à cette Eglise que Dieu a donné sa promesse: "Les portes de l'enfer ne prévaudront point contre elle."

"L'Eglise devant les évènements" pp. 5-8.

CHAPTER II

  1. Even the ecumenical movement needs a new burst of vitality and support: "...There is a grave danger that the movement will presently falter in its forward motion, and a supremely significant 'fullness of time' will pass unransomed." Albert C. Outler, The Christian Tradition and the Unity We Seek (Oxford: University Press, 1958), p. 8.
  2. "Life Through the Church," S. W., LI, 3 (1958), p. 237.
  3. S. W., LI, 3 (1958), p. 240.
  4. S. W., LI, 3 (1958), p. 238.
  5. In his criticism of the Social Gospel Visser't Hooft notes that in its theology "... an identification takes place between man's purposes and God's plan for the world. The old gulf which separated man from God is bridged and instead of a dramatic conception, that mankind is in revolution against its Creator, there comes the optimistic idea that there is a happy comradeship in the common undertaking of building a fairer, a brighter world. This can of course only take place because the relations between man and God have become continuous rather than discontinuous. It is believed that God and man do not live in two idfferent spheres of reality, which are separated because of the fact of human sin and which are only connected with each other when God takes the initiative in revelation or conversion, but that there is only one reality in which God may be described as the lengthening piece of man's aspirations. Or, to put it differently, a straight line runs from man to God. It is a matter of the intensification and strengthening of what we have and are already, not a complete break with everything in us, to come to God." Social Gospel, pp. 175-176.

  Visser't Hooft reproaches the Social Gospel to have rejected in fact the need for revelation. "It is evident that this conception excludes the need for and possibility of a special revelation. There is only one general kind of revelation, which may be more or less intense or evident in different cases but which is essentially the same whether we look to Jesus Christ or to ourselves. There is no qualitative difference between human and divine reality. The only voice answers man's cry from the depths is the one that he may hear in his own soul." Social Gospel, p. 177.
  6. The rediscovery of Christian ethics emphasizing social responsibility rather than individual morality remains the greatest contribution of the Social Gospel to modern Christianity and explains, at least partly, the vitality of religion in America. Because it represented the joint effort of the people of the Church, of clergy and laity, intellectuals and 'social workers',

social teaching of the Roman Catholic Church--namely Leo XIII's Rerum novarum or De conditione opificum, 1891--ever had upon Latin Christianity with the exception of France shere as early as 1871 'Le Mouvement Chrétien Social' and 'Les Cercles Catholiques Ouvriers', under Albert de Mun introduced a form of socialisme chrétien. In America the Social Gospel found its institutional expression in the Federal Council of the Churches of Christ in America, 1908 (later the N.C.C.). This led on the international scene to the Conference of Stockholm in 1925, and the formation of the Christian Council for Life and Work in 1929.

7. Karl Lowith, Meaning in History (Chicago: The University of Chicago Press, 1949), p. 3.
8. S. W., LI, 3 (1958), p. 242.
9. S. W., LI, 3 (1958), p. 243.
10. S. W., LI, 3 (1958), p. 245.
11. Cf. "Jesus Christ our Contemporary:" S. W., XXIX, 3 (1935), pp. 189-190.
12. S. W., XXIX, 3 (1935); L, 1 (1957).
13. The Kingship of Christ (New York, London: Harper & Brothers, 1948), and interpretation of recent European theology, The Stone Lectures for 1947 delivered at Princeton Theological Seminary.
14. Kingship. p. 17.
15. Kingship. p. 17.
16. In the second chapter of The Kingship of Christ, Visser't Hooft refers to Karl Barth, who in 1933 had remarked that "his fight against the German Christians had nothing to do with his political attitude to National Socialism and that the recognition of the powers ordained by God is self-evident." Quotation by Visser't Hooft of Die Kirche Jesu Christi (1933), p. 8 in Kingship, p. 48.
17. Cf. Hugh T. Kerr, A Compend of Luther's Theology (Philadelphia: Westminster Press, 1966) "An Open Letter Concerning the Hard Book against the Peasants," p. 213; "A Treatise Concerning the Ban," p. 214; "Secular Authority," pp. 216-221.
18. Institutes of the Christian Religion, Transl. Ford L.
19. Ibid., XX, 500.
20. Institutes, XX, 501. In regard to the practical aspect of this sovereignty see XXI, c.20 on "Civil Government." "The two 'governments' are not antithetical." p. 1487. "Necessity of divine sanction of civil government." p. 1488. "The magistracy is ordained by God." p. 1489. "Magistrates should be faithful as God's deputies." p. 1491.
21. F. Schleiermacher, The Christian Faith, ed. H.R. Machintosh and J.S. Stewart (New York: Harper & Row, 1962), II, 416
22. The Christian Faith, p. 469.
23. W. Temple had already reacted against the tendency. He did not want to ignore the theological contribution of the nineteenth century with its concern for the essential priority of man in the quest for truth and religious experience, but not at

the expense of the transcendence of the Gospel; "The Gospel does not begin with man's various needs and then offer ways of meeting them. The Gospel begins with God's truth, and calls upon men to live by it. A great deal of recent thinking about religion follows the other course. There is no harm in that, provided we do not force the Gospel into our mould. The philosophy of religion, and the comparative science of religions, are bound to start from the human end, for they must not make the assumption that the Gospel is the truth. If they reach that view at all, it will be at a late state in their proceedings, after much evidence has been reviewed. But the Christian is one who, on whatever grounds, has accepted the Gospel, and, so far as he thinks about it, is engaged in working out what is involved in that assumption." Christ's Revelation of God, p. 8. quoted by Albert E. Baker in William Temple's Teaching, (London: James Clarke & Co., 1950), p. 64.

24. Harnack, Wesen des Christentums, pp. 27-28, quoted by Visser't Hooft, Kingship, p. 28.

25. Ernst Troeltsch, Gesammelte Schriften, II, 522, quoted by Visser't Hooft, Kingship, p. 28.

26. Ibid., pp. 30-31.

27. Kingship, pp. 32-33.

28. H.R. Mackintosh in Types of Modern Theology (London: Collins, 1964) explains why Barth's theology has been called 'The theology of crisis'. Having noticed that for Barth 'crisis', at its profoundest, means judgment, he goes on to say: "to understand Revelation man must listen with the consciousness of standing at the bar of God." p. 254. On man's side this is indeed a point of departure in the experience of renewal. Cf. c.8, "The Theology of the Word of God, Karl Barth," pp. 252-304.

29. K. Barth once said to explain his concept of 'The Dialectical Theology': "Neither my affirmation nor my denial lays claim to being God's truth. Neither is more than a witness to that Truth which stands in the centre between every Yes and No. The task of theology is to interpret the Yes and the No, and the No by the Yes." (This use of 'No and Yes' goes back to Luther). quoted by H.R. Mackintosh, Types of Modern Theology, p. 255.

30. Kingship, p. 35.

31. Memoirs, p. 37.

32. "The Humanity of Jesus Christ," S. W., XXIX, 3 (1935), p. 232.

33. Speaking of that unique existence and of its significance in terms of reconciliation, William Temple, the champion of a world-wide Ecumenism, wrote in 1931 that "The Life of Christ is a momentary manifestation of eternal truth" or better that "The doctrine of the Incarnation is not first and foremost of importance because of what it says of Somebody who lived in Palestine; it is of fundamental importance because of what it tells us of the eternal and unchanging God, who is and always will be Himself; and if He, in His self-expression has given perfect expression of His character in terms of human life, then

as we look at that life we see the Eternal God." <u>Christian Faith and Life</u> (New York: MacMillan, 1931), p. 26.

In other words, discovering the authenticity of Christ's life, as revealed in the Gospel, depends in fact on a relationship of faith which transcends all theological formula. Indeed to accept the Gospel precisely means that by a movement of faith we discover in Christ the reality of God's existence.

34. <u>S. W.</u>, XXIX, 3 (1935), p. 235.
35. <u>Ibid.</u>, p. 236.
36. <u>S. W.</u>, XXIX, 3 (1935), p. 237.
37. Non, la foi n'est pas une chose simple ou evidente. Elle ne suit pas la ligne de moindre resistance. Au fond, elle est en oppositon a tout ce que nous voyons. Elle n'est pas naturelle; elle est surnaturelle. Pour arriver a une vraie foi, il ne suffit pas d'avoir entendu parler de Dieu et d'avoir accepté ce message comme on accepte un fait, il faut encore connaitre. Dieu comme notre Seigneur, savoir ce qu'Il est pour nous, et ce qu'Il veut de nous. Il faut entrer dans cette relation vivante avec Lui, dans laquelle on devient son fils obeissant. Et cela ne se passe pas sans un combat acharné. Cela ne saurait être une aventure ideologique ou sentimentale. C'est la grande crise de toute une vie.
'L'incognito de Dieu.' Les Cahiers Protestants XXII, 7 (1938), p. 406.
38. <u>S. W.</u>, L, 1 (1957), pp. 22-23.
39. <u>S. W.</u>, L, 1 (1957), p. 27.
40. <u>Ibid.</u>, p. 27.
41. The Cross means the end of hope to many who cannot see that without identification to Christ crucified there is no hope of resurrection: La Croix n'est pas une erreur de Dieu. Elle a la place centrale dans son oeuvre de salut. Saint Paul qui ne negligiait vraiment pas la Resurrection et qui pouvait écrire: "Si Christ n'est pas ressuscité, notre predication est vaine", a affirmé plus d'une fois: "Je ne veux pas savoir autre chose que Jésus-Christ et Jésus-Christ crucifié". Ainsi le mystère impénétrable de la Croix devient un message révélateur. Il révèle que Dieu dans sa bonté infinie ne s'identifie pas seulement avec nous, mais qu'il prend parmi nous la place la plus humble et que nous avons tort de chercher Dieu en haut, car il est descendu jusqu'au fond des abimes de la souffrance humaine.
L'incognito de Dieu, pp. 408-409.
42. <u>S. W.</u>, L, 1 (1957), p. 23.
43. Visser't Hooft wants above all to stress man's radical need and God's free initiative, but he does not want here to elaborate on the meaning of 'ransom': "We hear about ransom, and ransom means that something is paid to someone. We hear that we are bought with a price. We hear that we are redeemed, and the word redeemed also means that we are bought, and that someone paid the price for our liberation to someone else. Now it is quite clear in the New Testament that none of these words implies

that God is entering into a business transaction with us or about us. The question as to whom the price is being paid is really never specifically answered in the New Testament. In any case, it is not to God. He gives. He makes the sacrifice. Is it then to the prince of darkness, to the principalities and powers? At this point the New Testament remains extremely reserved, for the important truth it wants to get across is not to whom this price is being paid, but the fact that we are slaves, slaves of foreign powers, and that now these slaves are liberated, that they become again free for fellowship with God. In other words: none of these images that I have mentioned denies that the whole initiative is God's, that it is God's love which makes reconciliation possible and performs the act of reconciliation." S. W., L, 1 (1957), p. 24.

44. S. W., L, 1 (1957), p. 26.
45. Ibid., p. 27.
46. Ibid., p. 29.
47. S. W., L, 1 (1957), pp. 29-30.
48. Such confession constitutes "The Basis of the World Council of Churches," Section I of the Constitution accepted by the New Delhi Assembly of 1961. It reads: "The World Council of Churches is a fellowship of churches which confess the Lord Jesus Christ as God and Saviour according to the Scriptures and therefore seek to fulfill together their common calling to the glory of the one God, Father, Son and Holy Spirit." The New Delhi Report (New York: Association Press, 1962), p. 152.
49. Kingship, p. 73.
50. Ibid., p. 74. Visser't Hooft quotes Marcion here, but without reference: "In evangelio est Dei Regnum Christus ipse."
51. Kingship, p. 75.
52. Ibid., p. 79.
53. Kingship, pp. 80-81.
54. Ibid., p. 85.
55. Kingship, pp. 82-83.
56. Social Gospel, p. 46.
57. Kingship, p. 90.
58. "The People of God," S. W., XXXVI, 1 (1943), pp. 90-102.
59. S. W., XXXVI, 1 (1943), p. 94.
60. Ibid., p. 94.
61. Ibid., pp. 94-95, Cf. also Kingship, p. 91.
62. Visser't Hooft traces back the error of national socialism to the influence of Fichte, and he writes: "One of the first to proclaim the holy character of his people was the German philosopher in his 'Addresses to the German Nation' (1808). He was the spiritual father of the great cloud of witnesses to national religion, to the idolatry of the 'Volk'." S. W., XXXVI, 1 (1943), p. 99.
63. Reflecting upon Hitler's attitude toward the Jewish people in Mein Kampf, Visser't Hooft comments: "In the end it comes to this - that a nation which claims divinity cannot cherish any holy people in its bosom. It must protest against the Church

of Jesus Christ. The new ideology which seeks to transform the State into a Church cannot endure the existence of a community which by the mere fact of its existence reminds men that a people in the sense of race can never have the last word, and will not allow themselves to be absorbed in the totalitarian order." S. W., XXXVI, 1 (1943), p. 100.

64. The Church denies the Kingship of Christ when it identifies itself with the incarnation and by doing so it empties the preaching of the Word of all content. J. E. Lesslie Newbigin remarks in that connection: "If the Church is in itself, as an institution, the incarnation of God, then there is no need for it to point beyond itself to Christ - as true preaching must do." The Reunion of the Church (London: S.C.M. Press, Revised edition 1960), p. 61.

65. Kingship, p. 96.

66. He refers explicitly to Fr. Yves Congar's position in Chretiens Desunis (Paris: Les Editions du Cerf, 1937), p. 59, where the life and unity of the Church are regarded as an extension of the life and unity of the true God: "L'unité de l' Eglise est une communication et une extension de l'unité même de Dieu. La vie qui est éternellement dans le sein du Père, après s'être communiqué en Dieu lui-meme pour y constituer la vie divine celle des Trois Personnes de la Sainte Trinité, est par grâce, communiquée aux créatures spirituelles, aux anges d'abord, puis à nous. C'est cela l'Eglise; l'extension de la vie divine à une multitude de créatures."

Vatican II in the Decree "Lumen Gentium" still refers to St. Cyprian's famous formula, the Church shines forth as "a people made one with the unity of the Father, the Son and the Holy Spirit," (De Orat, Dom., 23: PL4, 553) The Documents of Vatican II, p. 17.

67. Kingship, pp. 98-99.
68. Kingship, p. 109.
69. Kingship, p. 119.
70. Ibid., p. 122.
71. Kingship, p. 123.
72. Kingship, p. 129.
73. Visser't Hooft, who had seen the Church in Germany in the 1930's and early 1940's, had no hesitation, however, to say soon after, in 1948: "After all, the world is not half as dangerous for the Church as the Church is for itself. The mortal danger for the Church is that it should cease to be the Church and not that it should be oppressed from the outside." Ibid., p. 129.

74. Ibid., p. 131.

75. Here Visser't Hooft refers to Quas Primas of Pius XI, 1925. Then he writes: "A Church which does not observe the eschatological reserve automatically transforms the priestly and prophetic Kingship into church-centered power politics. Its own existence and prosperity become more decisive critieria than the will of the King himself." Kingship, pp. 132-133.

76. Ibid., p. 142.
77. Kingship, p. 147.

CHAPTER III

1. Renewal, p. 34; with reference to I Corinthians 5:6-8; Colossians 3:9; Romans 7:6; Ephesians 4:23; II Corinthians 4:16.
2. Ibid., p. 37.
3. Cf. Henri de Lubac, Meditation sur l'Eglise (Paris: Aubier, Troisieme Edition), p. 91. Visser't Hooft quotes also the Report on the main theme of the Evanston Assembly. Cf. The Evanston Report (New York, Harper & Bros., 1955), pp. 70-72.
4. Renewal, p. 40.
5. Visser't Hooft comments here on the second and third chapters of the book of Revelation. Renewal, p. 47.
6. Timothy 3:5; I Peter 2:5; Romans 7:6; Philippians 2:1.
7. The fellowship of Jesus lives under the inspiration of the Holy Spirit; that is the secret of its life, of its communion and of its power. To use a word of Emil Brunner, the Spirit supplies the "dynamism" of the Ecclesia. The Misunderstanding of the Church, Transl. Harold Knight (Philadelphia: Westminster Press, 1951), p. 47.
8. Renewal, p. 39.
9. Renewal, pp. 92-93.

Visser't Hooft, early in 1930, shared his generation's need for a doctrinal understanding of the Christian faith. He wrote about the comprehensiveness of a doctrinal renewal of the Church. "Peut-être même nous faudrait-il entrer encore davantage en contact réel avec notre patrimoine doctrinal que nous ne l'avons fait jusqu'ici. Mais il ne faut pas que ce souci de notre passé devienne pour nous un moyen d'échapper à notre responsabilité présente. Il ne doit pas se transformer en retraite, derrière les grands prophètes et les grands maitres du passé. Dieu parle aujourd'hui et nous devons écouter Sa voix. Il ne doit pas nous suffire que Luther et Pascal aient compris Son Message; nous devons le comprendre nous aussi; Dieu est le Dieu des vivants; la doctrine chrétienne concerne un Dieu qui est notre contemporain, non notre ancêtre.

Nous devons rester en contact vivant avec ceux qui ont entendu Sa Parole dans les siecles passés, profiter de leurs enseignements, les écouter, nous appuyer sur eux; mais nous ne devons pas nous soustraire à nos responsabilités, en rendant un culte à la vérité qu'ils proclament, comme si elle était la vérité éternelle de Dieu Lui-même.

Doctrinal renewal to be authentic must be motivated solely be the desine to hear Theology speak of God: "un renouveau doctrinal n'est possible que si nous voulons une doctrine parce qu'elle nous parlera de Dieu. Des motifs apparement profonds, comme l'amour de la traditon ou le souci du message à offrir au monde non chretien, ne valent pas pour l'objet que nous nous proposons."

Without doctrine the Word of God soon looses its salt and becomes a word of man: "La Révélation signifie pour nous la

Révélation en Jesus-Christ. La doctrine est donc la transmission, la répétition de la Parole que Dieu nous a envoyée par Son Fils. Nous ne saurions nous en passer de la Parole de Dieu elle-même. Quand la doctrine disparait, l'Evangile est transformé 'selon l' homme'; il perd son sel, il devient une des multiples conceptions humaines de l'univers et cesse d'être le seul moyen constant de communiquer avec l'eternelle vérité." Signes d'un Renouviau Doctrinal. Le Seneux, XII, 8 (1930), pp. 509, 513, 515.
   10. Renewal, p. 91.
   11. Renewal, p. 97.
   12. Renewal, p. 18.
   13. Renewal, pp. 21-22.
   14. Ibid., p. 23.
   15. Renewal, p. 26.
   16. Renewal, pp. 35-36.
   17. Ibid., p. 41.
   18. Visser't Hooft quotes Irenaeus of Lyons and Origen as notable antagonists to that general trend.
   19. Renewal, p. 57.
   20. Visser't Hooft sees a crystallization of that position in Vincent of Lerins' Commonitorium. "Ut cum dicas nove, non dicas nova." Quoted in Renewal, p. 63.
   21. Renewal, p. 73.
   22. "The urge for reform did not cease when the reform councils failed. And it remained alive in the Roman Catholic Church even when it rejected Luther's Reformation." Renewal, p. 75.
   23. Ibid., p. 74.
   24. Visser't Hooft refers to the case of Pope Adrian VI, a Netherlander, whose brief reign brought hope. In 1522 he sent his numcio Chicregati to the Diet of Nurnberg, promising reform and a free council on German soil within a year. He promised also to give attention to the Centum Gravamina, or the Hundred Grievances of the Germans against the Church. He died soon after and was succeeded by Clement VII who supported the League of Ratisbon in 1524. In his instructions to Chicregati, Adrian VI recognized the sickness of the Church, the fact that the cleansing should begin with the Holy See itself for "the malady has crept down from the head to the members." The whole world thirsted for a real reform. CF. Yves M.J. Congar, Chretiens Désunis, Appendice II, pp. 355-356.
   25. Visser't Hooft refers to the Third Articles of Luther's Great Catechism to illustrate the point - also to Calvin's commentary on Isaiah.
   26. Visser't Hooft suggests three possible explanations of the failure of the Reformation; "One possible answer is of course that the Reformers did not meet with the response which they hoped for. [...] Another possible answer is that the institutional Church, indissolubly linked to society and the state in one vast Corpus Christianum, has been too strong for the Reformers. [...] There is another and more fundamental consideration. It is that the very message to which the Church owes its renewal

can be so misunderstood as to become an obstacle to renewal."
Renewal, pp. 79-80.

27. Visser't Hooft suggests that the expression originated in the seventeenth century; "Professor J. Lindeboom has found the phrase in the writings of Jodocus van Lodenstein (in 1674) where it is quoted as saying of 'a learned man' and in the writings of J. Kowlam where it is attributed to Hoornbeck 'following in the footsteps of Vaetius'." Renewal, p. 82, note 1.

28. Renewal, p. 83.
29. Ibid., p. 84.
30. Renewal, pp. 67-68.

"For the Christian, then, history is not the transient flow of time through static forms and institutions has for the ancient Egyptians). It is not the interplay of natural laws of balance and equilibrium in human affairs and the nemesis which brings down those who disrupt their balance (as in Herodotus). It is not an affair of chance, either, or of fortune (as in Thucydides and Polybius). History is not cyclical (as for the Stoics) nor the unfolding of some ideal structure of being (as in Vico and Hegel). Finally, it is not a fully managed puppet show, with God the puppeter." Albert C. Outler, The Christian Tradition and the Unity We Seek (London: Oxford University Press, 1958), p. 47.

31. "... we can say that the Christian sense of history must always include a sense of the mystery of the interaction between the really past and the really present, and so acknowledge that history is the arena of the action of God's Holy Spirit." Albert C. Outler, The Christian Tradition, p. 53.

32. Renewal, p. 69.
33. Renewal, p. 69.

Catholic scholars have traditionally been reluctant to accept the idea of a possible apostasy of the Church because of its identification with Christ and of the active cleansing of the Spirit. The Church is constantly and necessarily renewed. Daniel Berrigan, S.J., in The Bride, an excellent series of essays on the Church, claims that the Kingdom, as realized in the Church, never knows deterioration, for the triumph of the Spirit over all its enemies is guaranteed by God's promise. "Also noteworthy in the evolution of the Kingdom in sacred history is this: the process of inner deterioration, marking the course of all human enterprise, never occurs here. Across the broad face of history, and altering its features in spite of age and time and human defilement, comes the constant inner renewal which cannot be explained on any human grounds." (New York: MacMillan, 1959), pp. 124-125.

34. "The Threefold Christian Calling," S. W., LIV, 1 & 2 (1961), p. 28. In 1959 Visser't Hooft had published a book on the same subject under the title The Pressure of our Common Calling (New York: Doubleday). The book itself was based on the author's Taylor Lectures at Yale Divinity School in September 1957.

35. S. W., LIV, 1 & 2 (1961), p. 28.
36. Ibid., p. 28.

37. Ibid., p. 29.
38. c.4 "The Calling to Fellowship in Christ," pp. 63-78.
39. Common Calling, p. 63.
40. Ibid., p. 66. We find in the same chapter another attempt to define koinonia worth quoting: "Koinonia is, therefore, the way of life, the relationship with God and man which are characteristic of the community of those who are the objects of God's saving work in Christ. They are called into the Koinonia of Jesus Christ by the God who is faithful (I Cor. 1:9) and who constantly recreates and strenghtens the Koinonia." Ibid., p. 65.
41. Common Calling, p. 68.
42. Acts 15.
43. Common Calling, p. 69.
44. J. H. Oldham suggests the following definition of the Church: "The Church is thus the sphere of free relations of mutual love and trust between persons, and is meant to be the witness to the world of the true relations of men with one another." Church and its Function, p. 160.
   And Robert McAfee Brown proposes the following statement: "The Christian Church is a response to the 'good news' of God, proclaimed and enacted by Jesus Christ. Strictly speaking, it is not only a response to the gospel, it is a part of the gospel, since God desires not only to save men but to have them in fellowship with one another." The Significance of the Church (Philadelphia: Westminster Press, 1956), p. 39.
45. S. W., LIV, 1 & 2 (1961), p. 30.
46. S. W., LIV, 1 & 2 (1961), p. 31.
47. Ibid., p. 33.
48. Acts 1:8; Matthew 28:19.
"The Church is the community which has been gathered and mobilized by the Holy Spirit in order to fulfill that part of the plan of God which must be fulfilled in the final period of history. The whole Church is, therefore, at all times called to be a witnessing Church." Common Calling, p. 36.
49. S. W., LIV, 1 & 2 (1961), p. 34.
50. The mission of the Church is "wholly instrumental: says Visser't Hooft. The Church as herald or messenger of good news is not to proclaim its own ideas or impressions but the events of the Gospel. Cf. Common Calling, pp. 33-34.
51. S. W., XXVII, 1 (1934), pp. 75-81.
52. Ibid., p. 78.
53. Visser't Hooft writes in 1935, in Europe, against the background of Facism and National-socialism.
54. "Missions as the Test of Faith," E. R., XVI, 3 (1964) p. 252.
55. Ibid., p. 253.
56. Common Calling, p. 39.
"The relation of witness to unity is that churches which take their missionary calling seriously are given an opportunity to learn anew that the unity of the Church is an essential part of the Kerygma." Ibid., p. 40.

57. Ibid., p. 39.
58. Ibid., p. 40.
59. S. W., LIV, 1 & 2 (1961), p. 34.
60. "The royal office of Christ finds its ecclesiological equivalent not in ecclesiocracy--in which the Church rules the world--but in the diakonia attitude of theChurch in the world." Common Calling, p. 47.
61. Doctrine of complete separation of religious and secular society, each one living according to its own inherent laws. Cf. Gustaf Aulen, Church, Law and Society (New York: Scribner's Sons, 1948), c. 3, pp. 37-55.
62. S. W., LIV, 1 & 2 (1961), p. 37.
63. Ibid., p. 38.
64. Ibid., p. 39.
65. Common Calling, p. 47.
66. Ibid., p. 54.
67. Common Calling, p. 57.
68. "Material Need as a Spiritual Concern," E.R., XIX, 2 (1967), p. 229.
69. Renewal, p. 103.
70. Ibid., p. 103.
71. Ibid., p. 107.
72. Cf. "The Real Challenge of Communism," S.W., XXIV, 4 (1931), pp. 285-286. "Is Facism a Religion?" S.W., XXVI, 1 (1933), pp. 72-76. "German Protestantism at the Cross-Roads," S.W., XXVI, 3 (1933), pp. 256-259. "The Church in Germany," S.W., XXVII, 2 (1934), pp. 182-185.
73. "Theology for Churches in Times of Struggles", Address to A.S.T.S. Columbus, Ohio (1950).
74. Renewal, p. 111.
75. Cf. A History of the Ecumenical Movement (Philadelphia: Westminster Press, Second Edition 1967): Ruth Rouse, "Voluntary Movements and the Changing Ecumenical Climate," pp. 309-352. K.S. Latourette, "Ecumenical Bearings of the Missionary Movement and the I.M.C." pp. 353-355.
76. Renewal, p. 116.

CHAPTER IV

1. <u>Renewal</u>, p. 117.
2. <u>Renewal</u>, p. 120.
3. <u>Ibid.</u>, p. 212.
4. Cf. Jaroslav Pelikan, "Renewal of Structure versus Renewal by the Spirit," <u>Theology of Renewal</u> (New York: Herder and Herder, 1968), II, 21-41.
5. Karl Barth remarks in this connection that "the essence of the Church in the event of the divine Word and its human response is a single essence which is not divisible, separable, and which contains no inner contradictions. But it is just this essence of the Church in this event, in the uninterrupted current of its connection with the Living Lord, which is the one and only guarantee of its unity. Should this event come to a standstill, should the Church try to be the Church other than in the happening of this event, whould its eyes become sleepy, squinting, or blind, should it become an apparent Church, then its unity must be lost immediately." <u>God Here and Now</u>, Transl. Paul M. van Buren (New York: Harper and Row, 1964), p. 73.
6. <u>Renewal</u>, p. 121.
7. Visser't Hooft, "The Ground of our Unity," <u>The Nature of the Unity We Seek</u>, The Oberlin Report, edit. Paul S. Minear (St. Louis: Bethany Press, 1958), p. 121.
8. <u>The Unity We Seek</u>, pp. 124-125.
9. "The Outlook of the W.C.C." <u>Current Religious Thought</u> VI, 1 (1946), p. 14.
10. <u>Church and its Function</u>, p. 23.
11. <u>Ibid.</u>, p. 23.
12. <u>Church and its Function</u>, p. 23.
13. <u>Ibid.</u>, p. 24.
14. <u>Church and its Function</u>, p. 24.

Walter Marshall Horton Gives a rather comprehensive list of the points of agreement concerning the Church:
1) "All Christians are agreed in tracing the origin of the Church back to God's calling of a Chosen People under the Old Covenant."
2) "All Christians are agreed that the decisive act of God in the forming of the Church was accomplished in the death and resurrection of Jesus Christ, and the Church is in some sense the prolongation of this act."
3) "The Church is not only the People of God and the Body of Christ; it is also the Community of the Holy Spirit."
4) "Christians are universally agreed that the Church is a human as well as a divine institution."
5) "Christians are universally agreed that the Church is positively related to the Kingdom of God, but they are also agreed that she is not the Kingdom of God without qualification."

6) "The Church is charged by its Lord with a mission and a ministry in which all Church members are included and each is commissioned to some unique form of service."
Christian Theology, and Ecumenical Approach (New York: Harper and Brothers, 1955), pp. 210-215.

15. Church and its Function, p. 27.

16. Many catholic theologians today do emphasize the eschatological dimension of the community of salvation. Hans Kung writes: "... belonging to the Church is no guarantee, in this era of temptation, of belonging to the final Kingdom of God. The Church is not a preliminary stage, but an 'anticipatory sign' of the reign of God; a sign of the reality of the reign of God already present in Jesus Christ; a sign of the coming completion of the reign of God. The meaning of the Church does not reside in itself, in what it is, but in what it is moving towards. It is the reign of God which the Church hopes for, bears witness to, proclaims, It is not the bringer or the bearer of the reign of the reign of God which is to come and is at the same time already present, but its voice, its announcer, its herald. God alone can bring his reign; the Church is devoted entirely to its service." The Church, transl. Ray and Rosaleen Ockenden (London: Burns and Oates, 1968), p. 96.

17. Cf. The Documents of Vatican II, "Decree on Ecumenism," the whole section 22, pp. 362-364.

18. Church and its Function, p. 31.
Vatican II has not changed radically that position; cf. "Decree on Ecumenism."

19. Anglo-Catholicism and Orthodoxy (London: S.C.M. Press, 1933), p. 66.

20. Anglo-Catholicism, p. 49.

21. Anglo-Catholicism, p. 53.

22. Church and its Function, p. 39 (including quotation from A.M. Rainsey, The Gospel and the Catholic Church, (1936).

23. "...where the preaching of the gospel is reverently heard and the sacraments are not neglected, there for the time being no deceitful or ambiguous form of the Church is seen." Calvin, Institutes, XXI, p. 1024.

24. "...Holy Scriptures speaks of the Church in two ways. Sometimes by the term 'church' it means that which is actually in God's presence. [...] Then, indeed, the church includes not only the saints presently living on earth, but all the elect from the beginning of the world. Often, however, the name 'church' designates the whole multitude of men spread over the earth who profess to worship one God and Christ." Calvin, Institutes, XXI, p. 1021.

25. "...as the saving doctrine of Christ is the soul of the Church, so does discipline serve as its siners, through which the members of the body hold together, each in its own place. [...] Discipline is like a bridle to restrain the tame those who rage against the doctrine of Christ, or like a spur to arouse those of little inclination; and also sometimes like a father's rod to chastise mildly and with the gentleness of Christ's Spirit those

who have more seriously lapsed." Calvin, Institutes, XXI, p. 1230.

26. Cf. Calvin, Institutes, XXI, c. 12, more especially sections 5, 6, 8 and 9, pp. 1232-1238.

27. Calvin, however, affirms that the ministry of the Church is essential to "the renewal of the sainst" and to the edifying of the Body of Christ: "...neither the light and heat of the sun, nor food and drink, are so necessary to nourish and sustain the present life as the apostolic and pastoral office is necessary to preserve the church on earth." Ibid., XXI, p. 1055.

28. Church and its Function, p. 49.

29. "Various Meanings of Unity and Unity which the World Council of Churches Seeks to Promote," E.R., VIII, 1 (1955), p.20.

30. E.R., VIII, 1 (1955), p. 19.

31. Ibid., pp. 24-25.

32. The World Council of Churches has spoken on many outstanding points of church unity. Here are some:
(a) The unity of the Church is a given unity, in that it has its essential reality in Jesus Christ Himself (Amsterdam Report, p. 51; Evanston Speaks, S.C.M. Press, p. 18; Lund Report, p. 20, etc).
(b) That this unity must be made manifest to the world (Evanston Speaks, p. 19; Toronto Statement IV:2, etc).
(c) That full church unity must be based on a large measure of agreement in doctrine (Amsterdam Assembly Report, p. 55; "Christ the Hope of the World," p. 20; Edinburgh Report, p. 253).
(d) That sacramental communion is a necessary part of full church unity (Lund Report, p. 49).
(e) That a ministry acknowledged by every part of the Church (Lund Report, p. 26) and some permanent organ of conference and counsel (Edinburgh Report, p. 253) are required, but that a rigid uniformity of governmental structure (Lund Report, p. 34) or a structure dominated by a centralized administrative authority (Amsterdam Report, p. 127) are to be avoided.
(f) That the unity of the Church depends on the renewal of the Church (Lund Report, p. 21; Evanston Speaks, p. 23).
(g) That this unity is not to be sought for its own sake only, but for the sake of the world in which the Church performs its mission of evangelism (Evanston Speaks, p. 20; "Christ the Hope of the World," p. 20; "The Calling of the Church to Mission and to Unity," Central Committee Minutes 1951, p. 66).
List compiled by Visser't Hooft, E.R., VIII, 1 (1955), p. 22.

33. Renewal, p. 122.

34. Visser't Hooft refers here to Canon Gustave Thils. The Catholic scholar writes: "... il me semble que l'on peut dire que la plupart des communautés chrétiennes faisant partie du Conseil oecumenique défendent une conception de l'Eglise selon laquelle: a) La véritable Eglise du Christ n'existe pas aujourd' hui, quoad substantiam, dans une communauté historique determinée; b) en particulier, l'unité essentielle de cette communion historique visible n'existe point actuellement; les Eglises divisées

doivent 'devenir' l'Una Sancta, grâce au don de Dieu et à notre action unanime. L'Eglise catholique ne peut accepter cette position doctrinale." Histoire Doctrinale du Mouvement Oecumenique (Louvain: Warny, 1955), p. 173.

Cf. The 1st and 2nd Chapter of the II part: "l'Ecclesiologie du Mouvement Oecumenique," and "La Theologie Catholique et l"oecumenisme," pp. 125-205.

Cf. also "The Decree on Ecumenism," Documents of Vatican II, p. 346. Not only the Catholic Church is the historical Church--although separated communities are now recognized as churches--, claiming all marks of the true Church of Christ and re-affirming that "it is through Christ's Catholic Church alone, which is the all embracing means of salvation, that the fulness of the means of salvation can be obtained. It was to the apostolic college alone, of which Peter is the head, that we believe our Lord entrusted all the blessings of the New Covenant, in order to establish on earth the one Body of Christ into which all those should be fully incorporated who already belong in any way to God's People."

35. E.R., VIII, 1 (1955), p. 22.
36. Evanston Speaks (Geneva: V.C.C., Second Printing 1955), p. 11.
37. E.R., VIII, 1 (1955), p. 25.
38. E.R., VIII, 1 (1955), pp. 28-29.
39. "The Una Sancta and the Local Church," E.R., XIII, 1 (1960), p. 3.
40. E.R., XIII, 1 (1960), p. 4.

Visser't Hooft has always insisted on the necessity of searching for the gift of unity in the visibility of the Church. As early as 1935 he wrote: "Quand nous parlons de l'Eglise, tout depend du lieu ou nous nous trouvons. Et nous sommes toujours quelque part. Si nous voulons nous placer au-dessus de la mêlée ecclesiastique, nous nous trouverons en dehors de l'Eglise. On n'est dans l'Eglise que si l'on est dans une Eglise. 'On peut seulement être dans l'Una Sancta Invisibilis, si l'on est dans l' Una Sancta Visibilis, c'est-a-dire quelque part dans l'Eglise désunie.' (Karl Barth). Il n'y a pas de chretiens oecumeniques; il n'y a que des Lutheriens, des Reformés, des Catholiques romains, des Anglicans, etc. Ceux qui pensent avoir trouvé un terrain neutre ou supraconfessionnel, un point d'Archimède d'ou ils trancheraient la question oecumenique, montrent seulement qu'ils n'ont pas encore découvert l'Eglise réelle et qu'ils vivent dans le monde abstrait des idées et des theories, plutot que dans le monde des decisions concrètes qui est celui de l'église. Ils risquent de compliquer le problème oecumenique encore davantage en faisant de leur unité extra-ecclesastique une sorte de nourvelle petite Eglise visible. Notre point de départ, dans tout effort oecumenique, doit être notre Eglise" "Le Protestantisme et le Problème Oecumenique" Foi et Vie, XXXVI, 74, (1935), p. 617.

41. Visser't Hooft warns the protestants against the dangers of utopianism. In the article already mentioned he writes: "Je

sais bein qu'il y a des protestants qui pensent que le protestantisme consiste précisement à nier ce fait et qui saluent dans le mouvement oecumenique une occasion de se débarrasser de l'Eglise empirique et visible ou de s'enthousiasmer pour je ne sais quelle Eglise, irréelle et abstraite. Ils ont tort de se reclamer de la Réforme, parce que la Réforme a pris l'Eglise visible extrèmement au serieux et n'a jamais méprise l'Eglise visible au profit de l'Eglise invisible. Il est vrai, que Calvin n'ignorait point la difference entre l'Eglise empirique et l'Eglise de Dieu Luimeme. Mais il ne les separait pas, il ne les considerait pas comme opposées l'une a l'autre, mais plutot comme unité paradoxale. On a trop oublie ces accents ecclesiastiques chez les Reformateurs. Les protestants ont voulu être plus spirituels et moins 'catholiques' qu'eux; malheureusement, le resultat est loin d'être spirituel. C'est qu'ils sont souvent tombés dans l'erreur signalée par la Confession de La Rochelle en ces termes: "Nul ne doit se retenir à part et se contenter de sa personne.'" Foi et Vie, XXXVI, 74, (1945), p. 618.

43. E.R., XIII, 1 (1960), p. 7.
In fact it would be impossible for Christians to be a fudge of authanticity for God alone knows the true Church. "Souvenons-nous que, même si Dieu nous donne à reconnaître l'Eglise, le judgment définitif n'appartient qu'à Lui. Dieu nous demande de distinguer par la foi entre vérité et mensonge, entre vraie et fausse Eglise, mais notre choix restera toujours relatif. Dieu seul connait l'Eglise dans l'Eglise et l'Eglise en dehors de l'Eglise. De l'Eglise visible il faut dire avec saint Augustin: 'qu'il y a beaucoup de brebis hors l'Eglise et beaucoup de loups dedans.' C'est la grande réserve avec laquelle il faut procéder dans tous nos jugements humains. Notre tache est provisoire, comme toute notre situation chrétienne. Dieu nous demande d'aller de l'avant avec la foi qu'Il nous donne. Mais Il ne nous demande pas de prendre sa place." Foi et Vie, XXXVI, 74 (1935), p. 620.

44. Visser't Hooft, in 1960 before Vatican II, gave credit to the Roman Catholic Church for recognizing that there is a problem of unity. He wrote at that time: "The Church which has been most slow to admit this, the Roman Catholic Church, has just taken a considerable step in creating a new secretariate which is to deal with ecumenical problems. That does not mean that the Roman Catholic Church has changed its basic affirmation that it is the true church, but it does mean that it begins to take seriously that there are 'separated brethren' and that the relation of those brethren to the Una Sancta is a matter for serious consideration." Ibid., pp. 10-11.

This is, in fact, the essence of the Vatican II Decree on Ecumenism. The document is clear on two major points. It recognizes that Churches and Communities have been separated from full communion with the Catholic Church, which accepts them with respect and affection. Secondly, it reaffirms that unity, as of the esse of the Church, has been preserved only in the Catholic Church. "Nevertheless, our separated brethren, whether considered

as individuals or as Communities and Churches, are not blessed
with that unity which Jesus Christ wishes to bestow on all those
whom He has regenerated and vivified into one body and newness of
life--that unity which the Holy Scriptures and the revered tradition of the Church proclaim." "Decree on Ecumenism" the Documents of Vatican II, p. 346.
    45. E.R., XIII, 1 (1960), p. 12.
    46. Ibid., p. 11
    47. E.R., XIII, 1 (1960), p. 11.
    48. E.R., XIII, 1 (1960), p. 13.
    49. "Lausanne 1927, Faith and Order Official Report," p. 7;
quoted by Visser't Hooft: "The Calling of the World Council of
Churches," Report of the General Secretary to the Third Assembly
of the W.C.C. at New Delhi, E.R., XIV, 1 (1962), p. 220.
    50. "The Super-Church and the Ecumenical Movement," E.R., X,
4 (1958), p. 366.
    51. E.R., X, 4 (1958), p. 366.
    52. By monopolistic position one understand the medieval doc-
trine expressed by Boniface VIII in the Bull Unam Sanctam of Nov-
ember 18, 1302.
"By the words of the gospel we are taught that the two swords,
namely, the spiritual authority and the temporal are in the power
of the Church. [...] Whoever denies that the temporal sword is in
the power of Peter does not properly understand the word of the
Lord when he said: 'Put up thy sword into the sheath.' (Jn. 18:11)
[...] It is necessary for one sword to be under the other, and the
temporal authority to be subjected to the spiritual. [...] For
the truth itself declares that the spiritual power must establish
the temporal power and pass judgment on it if it is not good. [...]
We therefore declare, says and affirm that submission on the part
of every man to the bishop of Rome is altogether necessary for his
salvation."
Ray C. Petry, A History of Christianity (Englewood Cliffs, N.J.:
Prentice Hall, 1962), I, 505-506.
    53. E.R., X, 4 (1958), p. 372.
    54. Lack of freedom would weaken the Church as herald of the
Gospel. Elaborating on the characteristics of the Reformed position on Church Unity, Visser't Hooft remarked that: "The fact
that unity of the Reformed Churches is not sought by common sub-
scription to one or more specific confessional documents and that
most of them believe in the necessity of confessing the faith in
statements which give guidance to the faithful allow these Churches sufficient freedom to respond to new situations and to express
the one Gospel in categories relevant to each specific epoch or
culture. In our time of cultural pluralism this process of constant re-interpretation in terms of varying context is more indispensable than ever. It is especially necessary to encourage the
Church in Asia and Africa to translate the Christian faith on Asia
and African concepts. But since such 'accommodation' can only be
done adequately on the basis of a thorough knowledge of biblical
theology the Churches of Europe and American should stand ready

to help in this task. 'Relevant Characteristics of the Reformed Position' Bulletin IX, 4 (1969), p. 8.

55. Ibid., p. 375.
56. The Call to the Churches concerning the first Assembly stated: "Our first and deepest need is not new organization, but the renewal, or rather the rebirth of the actual Churches." Similarly the Assembly section dealing with Faith and Order at Amsterdam said: "Our churches are too much dominated by ecclesiastical officialdom, clerical or lay, instead of giving vigorous expression to the full rights of the living congregation and the sharing of clergy and people in the common life in the Body of Christ. We pray for the churches' renewal as we pray for their unity. As Christ purifies us by His Spirit we shall find that we are drawn together and that there is no gain in unity unless it is unity in truth and holiness."
quoted by Visser't Hooft, E.R., X, 4 (1958), p. 378.
57. E.R., X, 4 (1958), p. 384.
58. Ibid., p. 384.
59. Visser't Hooft defines pluralism: "a situation in which various religious, philosophical or ideological conceptions live side by side and in which none of them holds a privileged status." "Pluralism--Temptation or Opportunity," E.R., XVIII, 2 (1966), p. 129.
60. E.R., SVIII, 2 (1966), p. 130.
61. Ibid., p. 130.
62. Vatican II declares: "In view of the increasing international relations between people of different cultures and religions and for the establishment and strengthening of peaceful relations and concord in the human family, it is necessary that throughout the world religious liberty should be provided with effective legal safeguards and the supreme duty and right of man freely to lead a religious life in society should be observed." "Declaration on Religious Freedom," The Documents of Vatican II, p. 696.
63. "A Positive Response to Pluralism." Lent Talks. B.C.C. (1967), p. 2.
64. "... it is clear that for many years to come the main historic religions will be powerful factors in the world scene, that all of them are developing increasingly a consciousness of world-wide missionary responsibility; and that, just as Christianity has penetrated into their territory, so they will penetrate into territories which have been traditionally Christian." XVIII, 2 (1966), p. 132.
65. E.R., XVIII, 2 (1966), p. 132.
66. Ibid., p. 133.
67. Visser't Hooft writes: "In this regard it is interesting to note that in the early days of the ecumenical movement the ideal of 'the Christian society' still played a great role. The COPEC meeting of the British Churches in 1924 stated that it is in the medieval idea of the Respublica Christiana--a single, universal community, founded and governed by God himself, that the

authentic message of Christianity is to be looked for, at least potentially. By the time of the Oxford Conference on Church, Community and State in 1937 the climate had changed. [...] With regard to the old Christendom concept the conference spoke a sober and realistic word: "Today convinced Christians are everywhere in a minority in a predominantly unchristian world. [...] The Church has not yet faced the new situation with sufficient frankness. With the conservative instincts of all institutions of long standing and influence it has fought a defensive--and on the whole losing--battle for the maintenance of as much as possible of the old Corpus Christianum and the privileges and authority which that implies. But such a policy is doubly mistaken. First it is quite unrealistic. The younger Churches have never yielded such an authority, and for the older churches it is irrevocably gone, at least for the present era. Secondly, the ideal itself, though magnificent, was mistaken and premature. In practice it entailed more accommodation of the Church to the world than of the world to the Church."
E.R., XVIII, 2 (1966), p. 134 (with inserts from COPEC Report on International Relations, pp. 119-120; and Oxford; "The Churches Survey their Task," pp. 200-201.)
68. E.R., XVIII, 2 (1966), p. 136.
69. Lent Talks, p. 2.
70. Lent Talks, p. 3.
71. E.R., XVIII, 2 (1966), p. 139.
At the end of the Lent Talks already mentioned Visser't Hooft remarks: "... my point is that if Christians understand the signs of the times and show some real imagination, the pluralist society will be full of opportunity and lead to the renewal rather than the decadence of Christianity. The statistics may show that the number of Christians is going down in proportion to the population. The social and official position of the Churches may become much weaker than it has been. But the churches wake up and see their light. They will find a new integrity and therefore a deeper response.

Christianity was meant to be the salt of the world. The salt had become tasteless. The new situation into which we are entering can mean, must mean that the taste of the salt is restored." p. 3.
72. Ibid., p. 140.
73. Ibid., p. 140.
74. The Documents of Vatican II, pp. 676-677.
Visser't Hooft comments: "In this connection it is interesting to note that the final text of the Declaration on Religious Liberty of the Second Vatican Council contains on the one hand clear statements concerning the right of every person to enjoy religious liberty but on the other hand a most empatic affirmation that the only true religion is to be found in the Catholic and Apostolic Church. Many eye-brows were raised when this last affirmation was introduced in the last drafts. As a matter of fact it did not have much influence on the attitude of the opposition

for the number of negative votes remained unchanged. My own feeling is that wile the wording of this conviction is unfortunate in that it does not include the qualifications made in the Decree on Ecumenism, it is nevertheless useful to show that it is possible to accept pluralism as the pattern of modern society without embracing a religious or doctrinal relativism." E.R., XVIII, 2 (1966), pp. 140-141.

75. E.R., XVIII, 2 (1966), p. 142.
76. Ibid., p. 143.
77. E.R., XVIII, 2 (1966), p. 144.
78. E.R., XVIII, 2 (1966), p. 145.
79. Ibid., p. 146.
80. E.R., XVIII, 2 (1966), pp. 146-147.
81. Ibid., p. 147.
82. Ibid., p. 147.
83. Cf. the short "Declaration of the Relationship on the Church to Non-Christian Religions," The Documents of Vatican II, pp. 660-668.
84. E.R., XVIII, 2 (1966), p. 149.
85. Ibid., p. 149. Cf. also No Other Name (London: S.C.M. Press, 1963), pp. 113-124.
86. Visser't Hooft remarks that the word oikoumene occurs fifteen times in the New Testament. He recalls the use of the word in secular and Christian history. The word entered into ecclesiastical usage in 381 at the Council of Constantinople, which spoke of the Council of Nicea as an 'ecumenical synod'. The word 'ecumenical' acquired then "the special connotation of that which is accepted as authoritative and valid throughout the whole Church." The oikoumene is the Church Universal. For centuries the word was used in tis geographical and ecclesiastical sense. Curing the early decades of the Ecumenical Movement many churches rejected the word as a contradiction in adjecto because of the Roman Catholic Church's refusal to join in 'ecumenical' encounters. It was finally accepted in 1937 by the Oxford Conference and given its present meaning: "The term ecumenical refers to the expression within history of the given unity of the Church. The thought and action of the Church are ecumenical, in so far as they attempt to realize the Una Sancta, the fellowship of Christians, who acknowledge the one Lord," A History of the Ecumenical Movement, 1517-1948, Appendix 1: "The Word 'Ecumenical' - its History and Use," pp. 735-740.
87. Church and its Function, p. 95.
88. Karl Barth, The Church and the Churches, (Grands Rapids, Mich.: Wm. B. Eerdmans Pub. Co., 1936), pp. 15-16.
89. Church and its Function, pp. 91-92.
90. Church and its Function, p. 92.
Karl Barth writes: "The concept of toleration originates in political and philosophical principles which are not only alien but even opposed to the Gospel. Their triumph within the various churches was a sympton of inward weakness and not of strength." The Church and the Churches, p. 58.

91. The Church and the Churches, pp. 27-28.
92. Karl Barth, The Church and the Churches, p. 67.
And he adds: "If we remain on the level where confessions are divided, we remain where the multiplicity of the churches is inevitable." Ibid., p. 67.

Visser't Hooft warns the Churches against the temptation of overlooking convictions for the sake of activism, with its potential danger of "secular ecumenism." "The idea held by some people at the beginning of the ecumenical movement, that action unites whereas doctrine divides, and that we can therefore cooperate without asking fundamental questions, has had to be abandoned. The choices that we have to make, decisions that we have to take, depend on basic options. It is therefore to be hoped that the great possibilities for joint action will not prove to be occasions for yielding to the temptation of activism, but that on the contrary joint action will lead us to joint reflection concerning the Church's vocation today. More than this. The dynamic factor of which we speak must not be isolated from other factors, of which we will speak later. Today suggestions are being made, that ecclesiastical ecumenism should be replaced by secular ecumenism. Using different terminology for the same idea, certain people are saying that we are now entering the post-ecumenical era, for ecumenism was concerned about relations between Churches, but today the only important question is joint action in the world. I note in passing that this view of things shows a profound ignorance of the history of ecumenism. For the ecumenical movement has always had two dimensions: that of Church-unity and that of joint action in the world. But I am convinced that this conception of the ecumenical task is completely wrong. For if one stops working for unity between the Churches, one destroys the ground beneath one's own feet. Instead of entering history, one places oneself outside it. The world will really prove too strong for Christians without Churches, or in Churches which they do not take seriously.

93. Church and its Function, pp. 93-94.
94. Church and its Function, p. 98.

CHAPTER V

1. "Renewal and Wholeness," E.R., IV, 3 (1952), p. 385.
2. Ibid., p. 385.
3. E.R., IV, 3 (1952), p. 385.
4. Ibid., p. 386.
5. E.R., IV, 3 (1952), p. 387.
6. E.R., IV, 3 (1952), p. 387.
7. None other Gods (New York: Harper & Brothers, 1937).
8. None other Gods, pp. 3-4.

Commenting on man's refusal to choose, a trend of the day traced back to the influence of Andre Gide in the 1930's, Visser't Hooft quotes Pascal again then remarks: "You cannot do it. To be alive is to choose. The worst choice is the choice for pure drifting." Do not the facts bear out the truth of his observation? What indeed determines the lives of those who are so afraid of missing one of life's opportunities that they refuse to conalise it in any way. Our spontaneous acts are generally not the ones of which we have most reason to be proud. The poet who said:
>   Be yourself I said to somebody,
>   But he could not, he was nobody--
was really to generous for he forgot that there are worse things than our insignificance which may suddenly want to express themselves." 'We must Choose', The Intercollegian & Far Horizons. (1934). p. 31.

9. Visser't Hooft reacts against another trend, characteristic of the political movements of the 1930's, which would deprive the individual of such moral burden. "The other even more modern orthodoxy which would forbid us to make our choice among the possible philosophies is largely a reaction against the first. Disgusted with the spineless and sloppy kind of life which results from the "do as you like" school of thinking, it reacts to another and no less dangerous extreme by declaring that no individual can possibly choose for himself since the great life choices must be made for the individual by the collectivity of which he is a part. Confusing the individualism of egocentricity with the individualism of individual responsibility, it simply drowns the individual in the waves of blood, soil, race, nation or class. In some cases the choice of a private faith is left to the individual but at the same time it is made quite clear that the really ultimate and uppermost loyalty in this world is to be given to the god of the collectivity." Ibid., p. 31.

10. Visser't Hooft enumerates some of the ultimates man has to choose from: "If we take the most typical philosophies of our times we find three categories: first, the humanistic ultimates--human reason, human intuition, human well-being and others; secondly, the naturalistic ultimates--the laws of nature as the final authroity to which all must conform; thirdly, the

religious ultimates--God, however He may be conceived." Ibid., p. 7.
   11. None other Gods, p. 9.
   12. Ibid., p. 13.
   13. Ibid., p. 29.

In a brief article on "God? - or Religion," published in 1935, Visser't Hooft underlines the phenomenology of religion: "For what is religion? The word has two different connotations. In the first place it is being used as a vague conception to indicate a complex group of phenomena which have no other similarity than that they have something to do with man's attitude toward the deeper things of life. In this way it may include such utterly diverse matters as temple-prostitution and the Passion of St. Matthew by Bach or the man-eating ceremonies of some primitive tribe and the meditations of Pascal. The only implication in this case is that all these phenomena belong to a realm of life which differs from all other realms in that it is related to something which is considered ultimate. In other words, the only unity which is thought to underlie these "religious" facts is one of pure form and not of content.

But there is another way of using the word. Men were not content merely to classify and compare these phenomena. They made the attempt to construe more substantial unity out of the chaos and to discover its common denominator. And since the wish is often father of the thought the result was the idea that after all behind the weird incoherent mass of religious manifestations there could be found a "religion in which all men agree"--Religion with a big R, a unity not only of form but also of content." He then rejects the concept of Religion in the singular as an impossible dream. "The truth is that religion with a big R does not exist. There are only religions in the plural which cannot possibly be forced into one and the same pigeon-hole. If we were not so obsessed by the idea that it must be possible to organize the whole wide world into a neat and clear system of conceptions we would have ceased long ago to look for religion in the singular. For how could it possibly exist? If we attempt to unify the real religions, we find immediately that it is the things in which they differ and not the things in which they agree which they themselves hold most dear. It is of course possible to say that this is due to their intolerance and narrowness, but the fact remains that a synthesis between a Mohammedanism which ceases to consider Mohammed as the one standard of faith and life, a Hinduism which makes the doctrine of Karma an "elective," and a Christianity which gives up its faith that Christ is the unique revelation of God, is not a synthesis between these real and historic religions but merely between their pale shadows." The Intercollegian and Far Horizons (1935), p. 103.
   14. None other Gods, pp. 28029.
   15. Ibid., p. 30.
   16. Ibid., p. 33.

17. "The Inclusive and Exclusive Aspects of Christian Truth," S.W., XXII, 4 (1929), p. 350.
18. Ibid., p. 351.
19. Words attributed to Frederick The Great, quoted by Visser't Hooft in "The Inclusive and Exclusive Aspects of Christianity," S.W., XXII, 4 (1929), p. 352.
20. Ibid., pp. 352-353.
21. None other Gods, p. 23.
22. S.W., XXIII, 3 (1930), pp. 197-198.
23. None other Gods, p. 34.

For Visser't Hooft believing in the validity of scientific judgment should not exceed its own realm: "In our time, however, many are so naively obsessed by this particular mode of thinking that they do not realize at all that [scientific] the seemingly unshakable foundation of their "religion" is in reality as open to attack as the orthodoxies of historical religion. If they would only take the Marxists a little more seriously they would soon find out that there is no such thing as a religious position based on purely "scientific" evidence.

I do not want to suggest that all that goes by the name of religion today is necessarily due to this type of reasoning. In the first place it must not be forgotten that there are very many who are quite definitely Christian in their deepest assumptions and choices but who have just accepted the new terminology without realizing that it implies any change of content. And in the second place, there are many who are "religious" rather than definitely Christian, definitely Jewish or definitely something else, whose attitude is more determined by natural vagueness or undefined sentimentalism than by the logic of scientific rationalism. It remains true, however, that the frame work of modern "religion" is borrowed from a certain type of scientific monism which in the nineteenth century took the world by storm, which now is being attacked by many more recent philosophies but which is far from being definitely overcome." The Intercollegian and Far Horizons (1935), p. 104.

24. Ibid., p. 26.
25. Ibid., p. 37.
26. The Intercollegian and Far Horizons (1935), p. 104.
27. S.W., XXII, 4 (1929), p. 354.

Visser't Hooft, as we saw in the preceding chapter, has always been concerned with the problem of preserving the authenticity of the Christian faith in a pluralistic world. He raised the question in many articles. As early as 1934, he wrote: "...the question of Christianity's attitude to other faiths is at least as acute as the one of its attitute to irreligion. One might even ask whether, in view of the fact that man is such an incurably religious being, every secularism does not inevitably lead to some new idol-worship and whether therefore we should not take the positions of old or new faiths more seriously than the mere negations of secularism. However this may be, we are again deeply aware that Christianity is confronted with a situation in

which its very existence is at stake." "Christians and Other Pagans," S.W., XXVII, 4 (1934), p. 289.
    28. S.W., XXII, 4 (1929), p. 355.
Christ is the answer to the question of religion versus God: "If we would take Jesus seriously, we would abstain from putting religion in the center and God at the circumference. And we would not only do it by being Christian rather than "religious" but also by fighting the temptation which we have as Christians to be more interested in Christianity as a religion that in Christianity as service of God. The question, God, or Religion? not only addresses itself to the radicals and liberals among us but also to the fundamentalists and the orthodox. God not only is more than the Christian religion, he is even opposed to the Christian religion whenever that religion begins to be self-centered. There are forms of Christian piety which are as godless as atheism. In fact, every one of us is constantly tempted to make his own piety or obedience into a substitute for God and to live by the strength of his own religious experience or attachment rather than by the strength of God's gifts."
The Intercollegian and Far Horizons (1935), p. 10.
    29. None other Gods, pp. 48-49.
    30. S.W., XXIV, 3 (1931), p. 187.
    31. S.W., XXIV, 3 (1931), pp. 188-189.
    32. None other Gods, p. 53.
    33. "The Function of a Christian in the World," S.W., XXXV, 4 (1942), p. 257.
    34. S.W., XXV, 4 (1942), p. 258.
Speaking of the all-comprehensive aspect of the Christian calling Visser't Hooft stresses the dimension of grace of the Christian profession and the related moral responsibility. He writes: "So it is that the Christian's service in his profession must have the character of constant tension. On the one hand he must be a Christian and a doctor, a Christian and a teacher; he must be a Christian doctor or teacher. On the other hand he will never succeed in creating a synthesis between the demands of his service to God and those of his professional service in the world. In the world he is not a free agent; he is bound by the structure of society and of his profession. The decisive question is not whether he will be content with the solution of least resistance or whether he is ready to find the narrow way of decisions made before God. Caught as he is in the machinery of the world, he cannot act in the world as he acts (or as he knows he ought to act) in the Church. But that does not exempt him from choosing between obedience and disobedience. For there is a world of difference between the compromise which is the result of a real struggle, the effort to base one's thinking on the bible, a prayer for light, and that other compromise which is the result of cowardice and laziness." Ibid., p. 259.
    35. Ibid., p. 258.
    36. S.W., XXXV, 4 (1942), p. 258.

37. S.W., XXXV, 4 (1942), p. 259.
38. None other Gods, p. 49.
39. Ibid., p. 55.
40. None other Gods, p. 55.
41. Ibid., p. 57.
42. Ibid., p. 57.
43. Title of the fifth Chapter of None other Gods.
44. None other Gods, p. 61.
45. S.W., XXIII, 3 (1930), p. 199.
46. "Students and the Church," S.W., XXV, 2 (1932), p. 92.
47. S.W., XXV, 2 (1932), p. 92.
48. Ibid., p. 92.
49. None other Gods, pp. 65-66.
50. "Weakness and Strength of the Christian Community," S.W., XXX, 4 (1937), p. 289.
51. S.W., XXX, 4 (1937), p. 289.
52. Karl Barth has given seven notes of the real Church. They are worth quoting for they summarize Visser't Hooft's ecclesiology as well as that of Barth.
"1) The real Church becomes visible in so far as it emerges and shines forth from the seclusion in ecclesiastical organization, tradition and custom, in the power of the Holy Spirit.
2) The real Church will therefore always and everywhere be visible only to a very few, very frightened and very joyful 'Christians' and to these only by the free grace of God.
3) The real Church lives as the congregation of its Lord, i.e. as the assembly of lost sinners called by Him, and living by the consolation and admonition of the biblical witness to the reconciliation of the world with God, which has taken place in Him.
4) The real Church lives in the intimate association of those who are comforted and exhorted in this way, on the basis of their common relationship to the Son of God who was born, crucified and rose again as man for all men.
5) The real Church lives in the fellowship of the Holy Spirit, i.e. from the knowledge that the Kingdom of God has come, in prayer for the revelation of his Glory and therefore for the commission to tell all men that God was, is and will be for them all.
6) The real Church lives under the order and government which its Lord Himself exercises by endowing the congregation gathered in His name with the gifts it needs for the fulfilling of its service.
7) The real Church is the one, holy, universal, apostolic Church which we are invited to follow and be living members of, in that Jesus Christ calls us to be His followers."
Against the Stream, Shorter Post-War Writings, (New York: Philosophical Library, 1954), pp. 62-76.
53. None other Gods, p. 70.
54. Visser't Hooft remarks that "Catholicism as such has a great theory of the oneness of the Church, and classical Pro-

testantism has strong convictions about the Church as a community; but both have given way to certain spirits of the age--the first to the age of Roman external organization, the second to the age of modern subjectivism." None other Gods, p. 73.
    55. S.W., XXXIII, 1 (1940), p. 77.
    56. None other Gods, p. 71.
    57. Ibid., p. 70. In the last sentence Visser't Hooft makes allusion to the political situation in Europe in 1937.
    58. S.W., XXXIII, 1 (1940), p. 77.
    59. None other Gods, p. 76.
    60. Ibid., p. 76.
    61. Ibid., pp. 77-78.
    62. S.W., XXXIII, 1 (1940), p. 86.
    63. None other Gods, p. 79.
    64. Ibid., p. 81.
    65. S.W., XXXIII, 1 (1940), p. 85.
    66. E.R., IV, 3 (1952), p. 388.
Visser't Hooft gives many examples of the chain-reaction effect of renewal--from the Reformation period to the 'Confessing Church' in Germany in the 30's. He likes, however, to single out the case of Methodism: "Take for instance the Methodist movement. If you trace its genealogy you come across Martin Luther, whose preface to the Epistle of the Romans exerted such a deep influence on John Wesley. But you also come across the Moravians from Herrnhut in Germany whom Wesley came to know and to admire on his journey across the ocean. But behind the Moravians you find Francke of Halle, behind Francke the German Pietists, behind the German Pietists the Dutch advocates of practical Christianity, behind them again the British seventeenth century writers on personal edification. On the other hand the Methodist movement was one of the sources of inspiration of the widespread international revival movement at the end of the eighteenth and the beginning of the nineteenth century. At the same time that missionary and evangelistic revival was also indebted to Moravism influences from Germany. Scottish, English and Moravian contacts made Geneva into a centre from which many other Churches received inspiration. Basel became an energising centre for Germany and was in constant exchange with Britain. In the meantime several of these movements of renewal had also struck root in America. And later in the ninet-enth century American Christians took the lead in shaping the movement for missionary cooperation and the international Christian youth movements." Ibid., pp. 388-389.
    67. Actually, Visser't Hooft is quoting here but without reference. Cf. S.W., XXXIII, 1 (1940), p. 78.
    68. Ibid., p. 78.
    69. S.W., XXXIII, 1 (1940), p. 79.
    70. Ibid., p. 79.
    71. S.W., XXXIII, 1 (1940), pp. 81-82.

CONCLUSION

1. None other Gods., p. 78.
2. "Our Ecumenical Task in the Light of History," E.R., VIII, 4 (1955), p. 317.
3. Ibid., p. 317.
4. Cf. Stephen Neill, Men of Unity (London: S.C.M. Press, 1960), pp. 144-145.
5. Ibid., p. 145. Cf. also Robert C. Mackie, The Sufficiency of God, pp. 12-13.

List of Abbreviations:

The following abbreviations will be used:

    a. for reference to periodicals

S.W.	Student World
E.R.	The Ecumenical Review

    b. for reference to Visser't Hooft's works

Anglo-Catholism	Anglo-Catholicism and Orthodoxy
Church and its Function	The Church and its Function in Society
Common Calling	The Pressure of our Common Calling
Kingship	The Kingship of Christ
Renewal	Renewal of the Church
Social Gospel	The Background of the Social Gospel in America

    c. for reference to other works

Christianity and State	T.M. Parker, Christianity and State in the Light of History
The Christian Tradition	A.C. Outler, The Christian Tradition and the Unity We Seek
Institutes	J. Calvin, The Institutes of The Christian Religion

BIBLIOGRAPHY

The bibliography of Visser't Hooft's works is presented in three sections: monographs; S. W. articles; and E. R. articles- The latter two are arranged chronologrically - and other articles.

Anglo-Cathlicism and Orthodoxy, London: SCM Press, 1933.

The Background of the Social Gospel in America, Haarlem, Netherlands: H. D. Tjeenk Willink and Zoon, 1928; St. Louis, Missouri: The Bethany Press, 1966.

The Church and its Function in Society (in collaboration with J. H. Oldham), London: George Allen and Unwin Ltd., 1937.

The Intercollegian and Far Horizons, 1935.

The Kingship of Christ, New York and London: Harper and Brothers, 1948.

Memoirs, London: S.C.M. Press, 1973.

None Other Gods, New York and London: Harper and Brothers, 1937.

None Other Name, London: S.C.M. Press, Philadelphia: The Westminster Press, 1963.

The Pressure of our Common Calling, New York: Doubleday & Co., 1959.

The Renewal of the Church, London: S.C.M. Press, Philadelphia: The Westminster Press, 1956.

Articles and Editorials by W. A. Visser't Hooft in the _Student World_, Geneva: World Student Christian Federation, edit. Valdo Gallend.

XXII,	4,	1929	"The Inclusive and Exclusive Aspects of Christian Truth"
XXIII,	1,	1930	"Who Challenges Whom?"
XXIII,	2,	1930	"The Moral Responsibility of Intellectual Leaders - and Dr. John Mott."
XXIII,	3,	1930	"Do We Believe in a Personal God?"
XXIV,	2,	1931	"After a Year of Message Study."
XXIV,	3,	1931	"Preface or Epilogue?"
XXIV,	4,	1931	"The Real Challenge of Communism."
XXV,	1,	1932	"Wishing Peace but not the Means of it."
XXV,	2,	1932	"Students and the Church"
XXVI,	1,	1933	"Is Facism a Religion?"
XXVI,	3,	1933	"German Protestantism at the Cross-Roads."
XXVII,	1,	1934	"Notes on Student Evangelism Old and New."
XXVII,	2,	1934	"The Church in Germany"
XXVII,	2,	1934	"The Bible a Meeting Place"
XXVII,	4,	1934	"Christians and Other Pagans"
XXVIII,	2,	1935	"Catholics and Protestants"
XXIX,	3,	1935	"The Humanity of Jesus Christ"
XXIX,	3,	1935	"Jesus Christ our Contemporary"
XXVIII,	4,	1935	"The Life of Witness"

XXIX,	2,	1936	"Lord, Teach us to Pray"
XXX,	2,	1937	"The Federation in the Oecumenical Year"
XXX,	3,	1937	"The Church as an Oecumenical Society"
XXX,	4,	1937	"Weakness and Strength of the Christian Community"
XXXI,	2,	1938	"Christianity as its Own Adversary"
XXXI,	3,	1938	"The Messiania Secret"
XXXII,	1,	1939	"Order and Judgment"
XXXII,	2,	1939	"True Bread"
XXXIII,	1,	1940	"The Task of the Christian Community Today"
XXXII,	3&4,	1940	"The Church and Europe"
XXXV,	4,	1942	"The 'Function of a Christian in the World"
XXXVI,	1,	1943	"The People of God"
XXXVI,	4,	1943	"Natural Law or Divine Law?"
XXXVII,	2,	1944	"Social and Political Forces of Tomorrow"
XXXVIII,	3,	1945	"Our Way Through Ethical Chaos"
XLI,	2,	1948	"The Christian in World Affairs"
XLII,	3,	1949	"The Regeneration of Europe"
XLIX,	1,	1956	"The Bible in an Ecumenical Setting"
XLIX,	1,	1956	"The Bible and the Church"
L,	1,	1957	"Jesus Christ the Reconciler"
LI,	3,	1958	"Life Through the Church"
LIV,	1&2,	1961	"The Threefold Christian Calling"

Articles by W. A. Visser't Hooft in The Ecumenical Review, Geneva: World Council of Churches, edit. Eugene C. Blake.

VI,	1,	1946	"The Outlook of the W.C.C."
IV,	3,	1952	"Renewal and Wholeness"
VII,	4,	1955	"Our Ecumenical Task in the Light of History"
VIII,	1,	1955	"Various Meanings of Unity and the Unity Which the World Council of Churches Seeks to Promote"
X,	4,	1958	"The Super-Church and the Ecumenical Movement"
XIII,	1,	1960	"The Una Sancta and the Local Church"
XIV,	2,	1962	"The Calling of the World Council of Churches"
XVI,	3,	1964	"Missions as the Test of Faith"
XVIII,	2,	1966	"Pluralism - Temptation or Opportunity"
XVIII,	4,	1966	"World Conference on Church and Society"
XIX,	2,	1967	"Material Need as a Spiritual Concern"
IX,	4,	1969	"Relevant Characteristics of the Reformed Position"

Articles by W. A. Visser't Hooft in other publications.

Le Seneux, XII, 8, 1930.

Foi et Vie, XXXVI, 74, 1935.

Les Cahiers Protestants, XXII, 7, 1938, "L'incognito de Dieu."

Cahiers Protestants, XXIV, 3, 1940. "L'Eglise a la croisee des chemins."

Misere et grandeur de l'Eglise (Geneve: Labor et Fides - 1943)

Cahiers des Associations Professionnelles Protestants, 3-4-5, 1945, "L'Eglise et la mission actelle de l'Europe."

L'Eglise devant les Evenements.

"Theology for Churches in Times of Struggles, 1950.

The Cambridge Review, LXXV, 1822, (1953), "A Living Hope."

Aulen, Gustaf. Church, Law and Society, New York: Scribner's Sons, 1948.

Baker, Albert, E. William Temple's Teaching, London: James Clarke & Co., 1950.

Barth, Karl. The Theology of the Word of God, tr. G.T. Thomson & Harold Knight, Edimburgh: T. & T. Clark, 1956.

_____. God, Here and Now, tr. Paul M. van Buren, New York: Harper & Row, 1964.

_____. The Church and the Churches, Grand Rapids, Mich.: Wm. B. Eerdmans Publishing Co., 1936.

_____. Against the Stream, New York: Philosophical Library, 1954.

Berrigan, Daniel. The Bride, New York: MacMillan, 1959.

Brunner, Emil. The Misunderstanding of the Church, tr. Harold Knight, Philadelphia: Westminster Press, 1951.

Calvin, John. The Institutes of the Christian Religion, Library of Christian Classics, John T. McNeill, ed., tr. by Ford L. Battles, Philadelphia: Westminster Press, 1960, Vols. XX and XXI.

Congar, Yves. Chretiens Desunis, Paris: Edition du Cerf, 1937.

Cragg, Gerald R. The Church and the Age of Reason, Baltimore: Penguin Books, 1966.

Dillinger, John & Welch, Claude. Protestant Christianity Interpreted Through its Development, New York: Charles Scribner's Sons, 1954.

The Documents of Vatican II, ed. Walter M. Abott, tr. by Joseph Gallagher, New York: Guild Press, 1966.

Evanston Speaks, ed. World Council of Churches, Geneva: V.C.C., 2d printing, 1955.

A History of the Ecumenical Movement, ed. Ruth Rouse, 2d printing, Philadelphia: Westminster Press, 1967.

Horton, Walter M. Christian Theology, and Ecumenical Approach, New York: Harper & Brothers, 1955.

Jenkins, Daniel. Beyond Religion, London: S.C.M. Press, 1962.

Kerr, Hugh T. A Compend of Luther's Theology, Philadelphia: Westminster Press, 1966.

Kung, Hans. The Church, tr. by Ray and Rosaleen Ockenden, London: Burns & Oates, 1968.

Latourette, Kenneth, S. Challenge and Conformity, New York: Harper & Bro., 1955.

_____. Christianity in a Revolutionary Age, New York: Harper & Bros., 1958, Vol. I.

Lowith, Karl. Meaning in History, Chicago: The University of Chicago Press, 1949.

Lubac, Henri de. Meditation sur l'Eglise, 3rd. ed., Paris: Aubier, 1954.

Mackintosh H. R. Types of Modern Theology, London: Collins, 1964.

McAfee Brown, Robert. The Significance of the Church, Philadelphia: Westminster Press, 1956.

The Nature of the Unity We Seek, ed. Paul S. Minear, St. Louis: Bethany Press, 1958.

Neill, Stephen. Men of Unity, London: S.C.M. Press., 1960.

Newbigin, J. E. Leslie. The Reunion of the Church, London: S.C.M. Press, 2d ed., 1960.

The New Delhi Report, ed. W.C.C., New York: Association Press, 1962.

Outler, Albert C. The Christian Tradition and the Unity We Seek, Oxford: University Press, 1958.

Parker, Timothy M. Christianity and State in the Light of History, London: Adam & Charles Black, 1955.

Petry, Ray C. A History of Christianity, Englewood Cliffs, N.J.: Prentice Hall, 1962.

Pelikan, Jaroslav, Theology of Renewal, New York: Herder and Herder, 1968, II.

Schleiermacher, Friedrich. <u>The Christian Faith</u>, English translation of the second German edition, ed. H. R. Mackintosh & J. S. Stewart, New York: Harper & Row, 1963, 2 vols.

<u>The Sufficiency of God</u>, ed. Robert C. Mackie and Charles C. West, London: S.C.M. Press, 1963.

Temple, William. <u>Christian Faith and Life</u>, New York: MacMillan, 1931.

<u>Theology of Renewal</u>, ed. L. K. Shook, New York: Herder and Herder, 1968, 2 vols.

Thils, Gustave. <u>Histoire Doctrinale du Mouvement Ecumenique</u>, Louvain: Varny, 1955.

Vidler, Alec, R. <u>The Church in an Age of Revolution</u>, Baltimore: Penguin Books, 1965.

_____. <u>20th Century Defenders of the Faith</u>, London: S.C.M. Press, 1965.

www.ingramcontent.com/pod-product-compliance
Lightning Source LLC
Chambersburg PA
CBHW062012220426
43662CB00010B/1294